Pocket
REYKJAVÍK

TOP EXPERIENCES • LOCAL LIFE • MADE EASY

Alexis Averbuck

In This Book

QuickStart Guide

Your keys to understanding the city and its surrounds—
we help you decide what to do and how to do it

Need to Know
Tips for a smooth trip

Neighbourhoods & Regions
What's where

Explore Reykjavík

The best things to see and do,
by neighbourhood and by region

Top Experiences
Make the most of your visit

Local Life
The insider's city

The Best of Reykjavík

Highlights of the city and its surrounds in handy lists to help you plan

Best Walks
See the city on foot

Reykjavik's Best...
The best experiences

Survival Guide

Tips and tricks for a seamless, hassle-free city experience

Getting Around
Travel like a local

Essential Information
Including where to stay

Our selection of the city's best places to eat, drink and experience:

◉ Experiences

⊗ Eating

🍷 Drinking

☆ Entertainment

🔒 Shopping

These symbols give you the vital information for each listing:

☎	Telephone Numbers	👪	Family-Friendly
⊙	Opening Hours	🐾	Pet-Friendly
P	Parking	🚌	Bus
🚭	Nonsmoking	🚢	Ferry
@	Internet Access	M	Metro
🛜	Wi-Fi Access	🚊	Tram
✒	Vegetarian Selection	🚆	Train
📖	English-Language Menu		

Find each listing quickly on maps for each neighbourhood and region:

Bar Hemingway

16 🍷 Map p233, B2

Legend has it that Hemi self, wielding a machine rate this timber-pan ered bar during showpiece is a en by Papa ar town. Dress s.com; Hôtel Rit ⊙6.30pm-2a

---

Lonely Planet's Reykjavík

Lonely Planet Pocket Guides are designed to get you straight to the heart of the city.

Inside you'll find all the must-see sights, plus tips to make your visit to each one really memorable. We've split the city and its surrounds into easy-to-navigate neighbourhoods and regions, and provided clear maps so you'll find your way around with ease. Our expert authors have searched out the best of the city and its surrounds: walks, food, nightlife and shopping, to name a few. Because you want to explore, our 'Local Life' pages will take you to some of the most exciting areas to experience the real Reykjavík.

And of course you'll find all the practical tips you need for a smooth trip: itineraries for short visits, how to get around, and how much to tip the guy who serves you a drink at the end of a long day's exploration.

It's your guarantee of a really great experience.

Our Promise

You can trust our travel information because Lonely Planet authors visit the places we write about, each and every edition. We never accept freebies for positive coverage, so you can rely on us to tell it like it is.

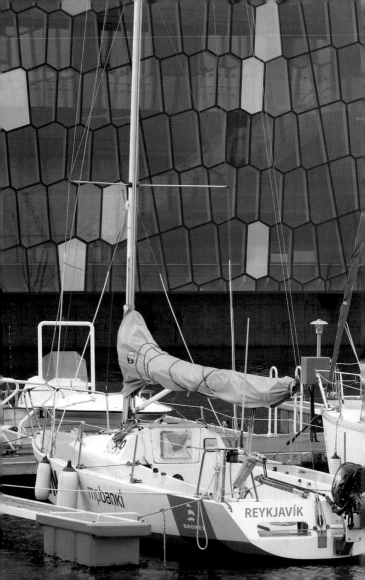

QuickStart Guide

Welcome to Reykjavík

The world's most northerly capital combines colourful buildings, wild nightlife and a capricious soul to brilliant effect. The quirky Reykjavikers embrace their sense of community and bring a joy to life, creating captivating museums, cool music, and off-beat cafes and bars. Reykjavík is a superb base for touring Iceland's natural wonders: glacier-topped volcanoes, shimmering falls and black-sand beaches.

Yacht marina at Harpa concert hall (p55)
RICHARD CUMMINGS/GETTY IMAGES ©

Reykjavík & Around
Top Experiences

National Museum (p24)

Iceland's National Museum gathers together the country's most priceless arte-facts, creating a trail of clues to life at Settlement and beyond. Peruse the finds and gain insight into the hardy hearts of Icelanders.

Whale Watching (p40)

Whale-watching boats depart from Reykjavík's Old Harbour in search of the magnificent leviathans diving, jumping and spouting off Iceland's shores. You might spot minkes, humpbacks, fin whales and more, plus diminutive puffins.

Reykjavík 871 +/-2: The Settlement Exhibition (p26)

The modern era meets the Viking longhouse at this exhibition centred around Reykjavík's oldest ruins, and souped up with fun, fascinating space-age displays.

Hallgrímskirkja (p50)

The capital's iconic church perches atop the city centre and is visible for miles around. From the heights of its modernist steeple survey the broad sweep of the city, ocean and snow-capped mountains.

Gullfoss (p80)

Thundering layers of icy water cascad over tiered rock faces and down an impressively narrow gorge at Iceland' iconic Gullfoss. Literally 'Golden Falls they, indeed, live up to their name when they sparkle in sunset light.

GUNTHER EGGER/GETTY IMAGES ©

MATT FRANKEL/GETTY IMAGES ©

Þingvellir (p76)

The continental plates part at historic Þingvellir, the site of the original (out-door!) Icelandic parliament. Waterfalls gush off the rift and ancient stones mark the earliest eras of Iceland's history.

Blue Lagoon (p70)

Wash away your cares at the ethereal Blue Lagoon, the flashiest version of Icelandic hot-potting. Set in other-worldly lava fields, with its vibrant geothermal turquoise waters, there's really nothing else like it.

Geysir (p78)

Iceland's impressive Geysir rises from a bubbling, hissing geothermal field surrounded by a contrasting lush valley. Like clockwork, one of the geysers makes a swooshing whoop as it shoots boiling water into the air.

Snæfellsjökull National Park (p106)

With its wild beaches, multicoloured lava fields and glittering glacier crown, the Snæfellsjökull National Park offers one of Iceland's best escapes – either as a day trip from Reykjavík or as a relaxing long weekend.

WESTEND61/GETTY IMAGES ©

Settlement Centre (p104)

Lively Borgarnes was the site of some of Iceland's most dramatic Saga action. Its Settlement Centre brilliantly recounts the country's discovery and settlement, as well as one of its most intriguing heroes, from *Egil's Saga*.

NATTACHAI SESAID/GETTY IMAGES ©

Jökulsárlón (p100)

A sparkling procession of luminous-blue icebergs shear off from Breiðamerkurjökull glacier and drift serenely through the 25-sq-km Jökulsárlón lagoon in ever-changing light, before floating by bobbing seals and out to sea.

◯ Reykjavík & Around
Local Life

Insider tips to help you find the real region

Reykjavík is small, approachable and charming, and in an absolutely gorgeous seaside setting, but its real magic is its people. A lively, creative, unself-conscious group, they live with inspiration and insight, they play hard, and they do it all with an easy aplomb.

Djammið Nightlife
(p52)
▶ Lively bars
▶ Partying with locals

Some visitors come to Reykjavík just for its nightlife. You may not realise it, but this tiny town can get out and party. The local name for it is *djammið* – a booze-drenched parade through the central Reykjavík streets, skipping from bar to bar.

Laugardalur
(p66)
▶ Geothermal pools
▶ Parks & gardens

One of the the favourite pastimes of Icelanders is a good soak and a chat at the geothermal springs. One of the largest pools, in Laugardalur, a valley of hot springs, sits alongside a popular spa, botanic gardens, bustling children's park and excellent local art museums.

Viðey Island
(p68)
▶ Secluded island
▶ Coastal views

Little Viðey Island, just offshore from Reykjavík, was one of the first spots settled in Iceland. Now an uninhabited, dreamy haven, it's dotted with unique art installations and criss-crossed by lovely walking and cycling tracks – a favourite quick getaway for Reykjavikers.

Reykjanes Peninsula (p72)
▶ Windswept Villages
▶ Volcanic landscapes

Yes, the Reykjanes Peninsula is home to the famous Blue Lagoon, but locals know it's also a land of fishing villages and lonely lighthouses, dramatic cliffs and migrating seabirds. You'll find Reykjavikers hiking or ATV-ing along its mineral lakes, volcanoes, beaches and rugged lava fields.

Laugardalur (p66)

Reykjavík nightclub

Other great places to experience the area like a local:

Reykjavík & Around
Day Planner

Day One

☼ Explore the historic Old Reykjavík quarter, taking in the **Ráðhús** (city hall; p31) and **Alþingi** (parliament; p31), then peruse the city's best museums, such as the impressive **National Museum** (p24), **Reykjavík Art Museum** (p29) or **Reykjavík 871 +/-2** (p26), built around a Viking longhouse. Lunch at hip **Nora Magasin** (p120), or grab a beer at **Café Paris** (p34).

☼ Wander up arty Skólavörðustígur, shop for the latest Icelandic music at **12 Tónar** (p63), then photograph the immense church, **Hallgrímskirkja** (p50). For a perfect view, zip up the tower. Then stroll Laugavegur, the main shopping drag, with boutiques such as **Kiosk** (p63) and **KronKron** (p63), or bookshop **Mál og Menning** (p63). Alternatively, take a dip at the **Sundhöllin** (p57) then examine the extraordinary **Icelandic Phallological Museum** (p55).

☾ Enjoy people-watching and drinks at **Bravó** (p61) or **Tiú Droppar** (p60) then go for dinner. Restaurants like **Vegamót** (p59), **KEX** (p60) and **K-Bar** (p58) turn into night-time party hang-outs, perfect for joining Reykjavík's notorious pub-crawl **djammið** (p52). Don't miss perennial favourite **Kaffibarinn** (p53) or beer-lovers' **Kaldi** (p52), and tag along with locals to the latest drinking holes.

Day Two

☼ After a late night out, brunch at **Bergsson Mathús** (p32), **Grái Kötturinn** (p58) or **Laundromat Café** (p33). Then head over to the Old Harbour (p38) for its museums, such as the **Víkin Maritime Museum** (p43) or **Saga Museum** (p43), and a **whale-watching tour** (p40). If sailing the open seas gets you hungry for lunch, grab a grilled fish skewer at **Sægreifinn** (p44).

☼ Visit **Laugardalur** (p66), east of the centre, for a soak at the geothermal pools, gardens, idyllic **Café Flóra** (p67) and cool art. Or ferry out to historic **Viðey Island** (p68), rent a bike and cruise its paths between art installations and fishing village ruins.

☾ Book ahead for a swanky evening at a top Icelandic restaurant, such as **Dill** (p57) or **Þrír Frakkar** (p58), then hit one of the new breed of cocktail bars, such as **Loftið** (p35). Alternatively, try out Reykjavík's most revered hot dogs at **Bæjarins Beztu** (p32), then catch a show at **Harpa** (p55), an Icelandic movie at **Bíó Paradís** (p62) or live music at **Café Rosenberg** (p62).

Short on time?
We've arranged Reykjavík's must-sees into these day-by-day itineraries to make sure you see the very best of the city and its surrounds in the time you have available.

Day Three

If you've got the time and can rent your own wheels, you can extend these country loops. Day tours are also a popular, effective option. Get an early start with the famous **Golden Circle** (p74). Explore the rift and historic parliament site **Þingvellir** (p76) then lunch in Laugarvatn on delicious local fare at **Lindin** (p86).

Zip to spouting **Geysir** (p78) and cascading **Gullfoss** (p80), leaving time for **river rafting** (p86) out of Reykholt or a soak at the natural, restored spring at **Gamla Laugin** (p83) in Flúðir. Alternatively, roam the **Þjórsárdalur** (p89), a broad volcanic river valley with a handful of disparate sights including a Settlement Era farmstead, hidden waterfalls and the foothills of Hekla volcano.

If you're tired, head home, stopping for dinner at **Tryggvaskála** (p87) in Selfoss or **Varma** (p87) in Hveragerði. If not, use your car to go to the shore for seafood at sleepy fishing villages **Stokkseyri** and **Eyrarbakki** (p92). Or, if you haven't the time to visit the **Blue Lagoon** (p71) coming or going from the airport, go late this evening, after the crowds have dwindled, before returning to Reykjavík.

Day Four

Choose between the wonderful west or the famous south. If you're going to west Iceland, spend the morning at Borgarnes' **Settlement Centre** (p104) learning about Icelandic history and *Egil's Saga*. If you're heading south, drive to Hella or Hvolsvöllur for **horse riding** (p93), or zoom all the way to **Skógar** (p89) via its marvellous falls **Seljalandsfoss & Gljúfurárbui** (p95). Catch an amphibious bus or join a super-Jeep trip to **Þórsmörk** (p99), a forested valley, or take a guided walk on **Sólheimajökull** (p95).

In the west, choose between exploring inland lava tubes at **Viðgelmir** (p111) and the interior of a glacier at **Langjökull Ice Cave** (p111), or hiking, whale watching and glacier walking in **Snæfellsjökull National Park** (p106). In the south, shoot out to Vík for black basalt beach **Reynisfjara** (p92) and enormous rock arch landmark **Dyrhólaey** (p92).

In the west, finish in Stykkishólmur with dinner at **Plássið** (p114) or **Narfeyrarstofa** (p113). In the south, barrel up the northeast coast, through otherworldly rocky deltas and grand buttes, to the incredible glacier tongues descending from **Vatnajökull** (p96), and fantastical glacier lagoon **Jökulsárlón** (p100).

Need to Know

For more information,
see Survival Guide (p137)

Currency
Icelandic króna (Ikr)

Language
Icelandic; English widely spoken

Visas
Generally not required for stays of up to 90 days. Member of the Schengen Convention.

Money
Credit cards reign supreme, even in the most rural reaches of the country (PIN required for some purchases, such as petrol). ATMs available in all towns.

Mobile Phones
Mobile coverage widespread. Visitors with GSM phones can make roaming calls; purchase a local SIM card if you're staying awhile.

Time
Western European Time Zone (GMT/UTC, same as London)

Plugs & Adaptors
Plugs have two round pins; electrical current is 220V. North American visitors require an adaptor, and for non-compatible gadgets, a transformer.

Tipping
As service and VAT (value-added tax) are always included in prices, tipping isn't required in Iceland.

① Before You Go

Your Daily Budget

Budget less than Ikr20,000
▶ Dorm bed Ikr4000–7000
▶ Grill-bar grub/soup lunch Ikr1200–1800
▶ Golden Circle bus pass Ikr8500

Midrange Ikr20,000–35,000
▶ Guesthouse double room Ikr17,000–25,000
▶ Cafe meal Ikr1800–3000
▶ Small vehicle rental Ikr14,000

Top End more than Ikr35,000
▶ Boutique double room Ikr30,000–50,000
▶ Main dish in top restaurant Ikr4000–7000
▶ 4WD rental Ikr30,000

Useful Websites

Visit Iceland (www.visiticeland.com) Official tourism portal.

Visit Reykjavík (www.visitreykjavik.is) Official capital site.

Reykjavík Grapevine (www.grapevine.is) Great English-language newspaper/website.

Iceland Review (www.icelandreview.com) News, current affairs, entertainment and more.

Lonely Planet (www.lonelyplanet.com/iceland) Destination information, traveller forum and more.

Advance Planning

Three to six months before Book all accommodation in Reykjavík and beyond. Demand always outstrips supply.

One month before Book adventure or bus tours in the countryside.

One week before Reserve tables at top restaurants. Prebook airport bus if you want to hit the Blue Lagoon on arrival.

2 Arriving in Reykjavík

Iceland's primary international airport, Keflavík International Airport (KEF) is 48km west of Reykjavík, on the Reykjanes Peninsula. Frequent, convenient buses serve central Reykjavík.

✈ From Keflavík International Airport

Bus Flybus (📞580 5400; www.re.is; 📶), Airport Express (📞540 1313; www.airportexpress.is; 📶) and discount operator K-Express (📞823 0099; www.kexpress.is), whose stop is off-terminal, have buses connecting the airport with Reykjavík (50 minutes). Flybus offers pick-up/drop-off at many accommodations (Ikr1950 to Reykjavík, Ikr2500 to hotel), and also serves the Blue Lagoon.

Destination	Best Transport
Central Reykjavík	Flybus, Airport Express, K-Express
Blue Lagoon	Flybus: Blue Lagoon

✈ At the Airport

Keflavík International Airport The airport has ATMs, money exchange, car hire, an information desk and cafes. The duty-free shops in the arrival area sell liquor at far better prices than you'll find in town. There's also a desk for collecting duty-free cash back from eligible purchases in Iceland. The 10-11 convenience store sells SIM cards, and major car companies like Reykjavík Excursions and Grey Line have desks.

3 Getting Around

A car is unnecessary in central Reykjavík as it's so easy to explore on foot and by bus. Car and camper hire are best for countryside excursions.

🚌 Local Bus

Strætó (📞540 2700; www.straeto.is) operates regular, easy buses around Reykjavík and its suburbs; it also operates long-distance buses (p141). It has online schedules, a smartphone app and a route book for sale at Hlemmur bus station (Ikr0.50). Many free maps like the *Welcome to Reykjavík City Map* also include bus-route maps.

The fare is Ikr350 and can be paid on board (no change given). Buses run from 7am until 11pm or midnight daily (from 10am on Sunday). A limited night-bus service runs until 2am on Friday and Saturday.

🚗 Car

The most common way for visitors to get around outside of Reykjavík, cars are pricey to hire but provide great freedom. A 2WD vehicle will get you almost everywhere in summer (note: not into the highlands, or on F roads). Summer-only 4WD buses go to the highlands, or you'll need a 4WD or a tour. Cars are available at both airports, the BSÍ bus terminal and some city locations.

🚌 Regional Bus

Iceland has a decent bus network operating from around mid-May to mid-September between major destinations. Outside these months services are less frequent (or nonexistent).

✈ Regional Flights

If you're short on time, domestic flights can help you maximise your stay.

Reykjavík & Around
Neighbourhoods

Whale Watching ◉

◉ **Reykjavík 871+/-2: The Settlement Exhibition**

Old Harbour (p38)
Once primarily a working harbour, this pretty, lively district now offers a fun cluster of museums and eateries, and is the launch-point for whale-watching boats.

◉ **Top Experiences**

Whale Watching

Old Reykjavík (p22)
Reykjavík's ancient heart lies here, with its remains of a Viking longhouse, interesting architecture and top museums.

◉ **Top Experiences**

National Museum

Reykjavík 871 +/-2: The Settlement Exhibition

◉ **National Museum**

Laugavegur & Skólavörðustígur (p48)

Laugavegur is Reykjavík's premier shopping street and centre for cool cafes, bars and restaurants. Its arty cousin Skólavörðustígur leads to famous Hallgrímskirkja.

◉ Top Experiences

Hallgrímskirkja

Golden Circle (p74)

◉ Top Experiences

Þingvellir

Geysir

Gullfoss

West Iceland (p102)

◉ Top Experiences

Settlement Centre

Snæfellsjökull National Park

South Coast (p88)

Worth a Trip

◉ Top Experiences

Blue Lagoon

Jökulsárlón

Hallgrímskirkja

Explore
Reykjavík

Worth a Trip

View over Reykjavík from Hallgrímskirkja (p50)
TSUGULIEV/SHUTTERSTOCK ©

Explore

Old Reykjavík

The area dubbed Old Reykjavík is the jaunty heart of the capital. Anchored by placid Tjörnin, the city-centre lake, the neighbourhood is loaded with brightly coloured residential houses and a series of great sights and interesting historic buildings. Old Reykjavík is also tops for a wander: from the seafront to Austurvöllur park, Alþingi (parliament) and Ráðhús (city hall) and on to the National Museum.

Experiences in a Day

☀ Get an early start at the **Reykjavík Art Museum – Hafnarhús** (p29) or the **Reykjavík Museum of Photography** (p31) for the city's best contemporary art, then stroll up through the oldest parts of town around **Austurvöllur** (p31), where you'll find the **Alþingi** (p31) and **Ráðhús** (p31) on the edge of pretty **Tjörnin** (p29) lake. Visit the Viking longhouse and high-tech exhibits at **Reykjavík 871 +/-2** (p26) before heading to lunch at **Bergsson Mathús** (p32) or **Nora Magasin** (p32).

☀ Walk through the lake's parks or hop a bus to reach the absorbing **National Museum** (p24). Spend the afternoon perusing the country's most precious artefacts, while learning about its history.

☾ Head back to the centre for a fantastic dinner at **Grill-markaðurinn** (p32) or a casual meal at **Laundromat Café** (p33), then tip back brews at **Micro Bar** (p35) or dress up for fine cocktails at **Loftið** (p35). Catch live bands at **Húrra** (p36), before late-night dancing at **Paloma** (p35) or nightcap hot dogs at **Bæjarins Beztu** (p32).

👁 Top Experiences

National Museum (p24)

Reykjavík 871 +/-2: The Settlement Exhibition (p26)

💙 Best of Reykjavík

Eating

Grillmarkaðurinn (p32)

Fiskfélagið (p32)

Fiskmarkaðurinn (p34)

Bæjarins Beztu (p32)

Museums, Exhibitions & Galleries

National Museum (p24)

Reykjavík 871 +/-2: The Settlement Exhibition (p26)

Reykjavík Art Museum – Hafnarhús (p29)

Reykjavík Museum of Photography (p31)

Getting There

✪ **On Foot** Central Reykjavík is super-compact and walkable. You'll get to most places on foot.

🚌 **Bus** City buses 1, 3, 6, 12 and 14 from Hlemmur all stop in Old Reykjavík at Lækjartorg and Ráðhús.

🚌 **Bus** Bus 12 connects Laugardalur, Hlemmur and Old Reykjavík, as does bus 14, which also goes to the Old Harbour.

Top Experiences
National Museum

The superb National Museum beautifully displays artefacts from Settlement to the modern age that have been collected from all over Iceland. Whether you come at the beginning or the end of your trip, this museum provides a meaningful overview of Iceland's history and culture. Brilliantly curated displays lead you through the struggle to settle and organise the forbidding island, the radical changes wrought by the advent of Christianity, the lean times of domination by foreign powers and Iceland's eventual independence.

👁 Map p28, A5

📞 530 2200

www.nationalmuseum.is

Suðurgata 41

adult/child Ikr1500/free

🕑 10am-5pm May–mid-Sep, 11am-5pm Tue-Sun mid-Sep–Apr

Don't Miss

Settlement Era Finds

The premier section of the museum describes the Settlement Era, and features swords, meticulously carved **drinking horns**, and **silver hoards**. A powerful **bronze figure of Thor** is thought to date to about 1000.

Domestic Life

Exhibits explain how the chieftains ruled and how people survived on little, lighting their dark homes and fashioning bog iron. There's everything from the remains of early *skyr* production to intricate pendants and broaches. Look for the Viking-era **hnefatafl game set** (a bit like chess); this artefact's discovery in a grave in Baldursheimar led to the founding of the museum.

Viking Graves

Encased in the floor, you'll find Viking-era graves, with their precious burial goods: horse bones, a sword, pins, a ladle, a comb. One of the tombs containing an 8-month-old infant is the only one of its kind ever found.

Ecclesiastical Artefacts

The section of the museum that details the introduction of Christianity is chock-a-block with rare art and artefacts. For example, the priceless 13th-century **Valþjófsstaðir church door**.

The Modern Era

Upstairs, collections span from 1600 to today and give a clear sense of how Iceland struggled under foreign rule, finally gained independence, and went on to modernise. Look for the **papers and belongings of Jón Sigurðsson**, the architect of Iceland's independence.

☑ **Top Tips**

▸ The excellent audioguide (Ikr300) adds loads of useful detail. The one for kids is in Icelandic or English only.

▸ Free English tours are run at 11am on Wednesdays, Saturdays and Sundays from mid-May to September.

▸ Leave a little extra time for the museum's rotating photographic exhibitions.

▸ It's a bit out of the way; hop on bus 1, 3, 6, 12 or 14 to reach the museum.

✕ **Take a Break**

The museum's ground-floor cafe offers wi-fi and a welcome respite, with wraparound windows looking out on a flowing fountain. It serves a full range of coffee drinks and wholesome soups, sandwiches and salads (snacks Ikr600 to Ikr1600).

Otherwise, you'll need to hop a bus back into the centre for food.

Top Experiences
Reykjavík 871 +/-2: The Settlement Exhibition

This fascinating archaeological ruin-museum is based around a 10th-century Viking longhouse and other Settlement Era finds from central Reykjavík. The museum's name comes from the estimated date of the tephra layer beneath the longhouse (the year 871, plus or minus two years). Fine exhibitions imaginatively combine technological wizardry and archaeology to give a glimpse into early Icelandic life. Excavations in the area are ongoing and on-site curators and archaeo-anthropologists have a passion for bringing history to life.

👁 Map p28, B2

📞 411 6370

www.reykjavikmuseum.is

Aðalstræti 16

adult/child Ikr1300/free

🕙 10am-5pm, English-language tour 11am Mon, Wed & Fri Jun-Aug

Don't Miss

Viking Longhouse

The entire museum is constructed around a 10th-century Viking longhouse unearthed here on Aðalstræti from 2001 to 2002. Mainly a series of foundation walls now, it was thought to be inhabited for only 60 years. Things to look out for are areas with animal bones deliberately built into the structure (for good fortune, perhaps), and the old spring.

Boundary Wall

Tephra layers are the layer of fragments from a volcanic eruption, and are used to date sites around Iceland. The longhouse was built on top of the 871 layer, but don't miss the fragment of boundary wall at the back of the museum, which was found *below* the tephra layer, and is thus older still. It's the oldest human-made structure in Reykjavík.

Ancient Artefacts

Arcing around the side of the exhibit, softly lit niches contain artefacts found in the area, ranging from great auk bones (the bird is now extinct) to fish oil lamps and an iron axe. The latest finds from ancient workshops near the current Alþingi include a silver bracelet and a spindle whorl (for making thread) inscribed with runes (reading 'Vilborg owns me').

High-Tech Displays

Among the captivating high-tech displays are interactive multimedia tables explaining the area's excavations, which span several city blocks; a wraparound panorama showing how things would have looked at the time of the longhouse; and a space-age-feeling panel that allows you to steer through different layers of the longhouse's construction.

☑ Top Tips

▶ Excellent English-language tours run at 11am Monday, Wednesday and Friday from June to August.

▶ Multilingual audio-guides are free.

▶ The museum's fun kids' corner has traditional Icelandic toys, rune spelling exercises and computer games.

▶ Museum entry is part of a joint ticket with **Árbæjarsafn** (www.reykjavikmuseum.is; Kistuhylur 4, Ártúnsholt; adult/child Ikr1300/free; ⏰10am-5pm Jun-Aug, by tour only 1pm Mon-Fri Sep-May; 🚼; 🚌12, 19, 24) open-air museum, 4km east of the centre.

✗ Take a Break

Stroll up to Tjörnin to the lakeside city hall, inside of which Við Tjörnina (p33) is a relaxing cafe-restaurant with views to the water. Or, head to the Austurvöllur square area, where cafes and bars such as Café Paris (p34) spill onto the park in warmer months.

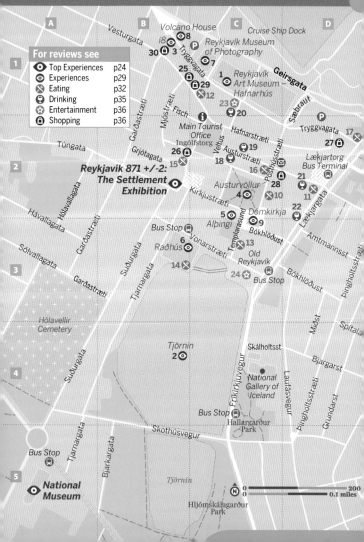

Vesturgata

Volcano House

Cruise Ship Dock

i8

8

30 3 Tryggvagata

7

Reykjavík Museum of Photography

Geirsgata

25

1 Reykjavík Art Museum – Hafnarhús

Sæbraut

29

12

23

20

For reviews see

Top Experiences	p24
Experiences	p29
Eating	p32
Drinking	p35
Entertainment	p36
Shopping	p36

Garðastræti

Mjóstræti

Fisch

Main Tourist Office

Hafnarstræti

Tryggvagata

17

27

Lækjartorg Bus Terminal

Túngata

Ingólfstorg

Grjótagata

26

15

18

Veltus

19

Austurstræti

16

21

11

28

10

Reykjavík 871 +/-2: The Settlement Exhibition

Kirkjustræti

Austurvöllur

4

22

Lækjargata

Hávallagata

Hólavallagata

Dómkirkja

5

Alþingi

9

Bus Stop

Amtmannsst

Sólvallagata

Suðurgata

Tjarnagata

6

Ráðhús

Vonarstræti

Bókhlöðust

13

Old Reykjavík

Garðastræti

14

24

Bus Stop

Bókhlöðust

Þingholtsstræti

Hólavellir Cemetery

Miðst

Spítala

Tjörnin

2

Skálholtsst

Bjargarst

National Gallery of Iceland

Suðurgata

Friðrikjuvegur

Laufásvegur

Þingholtsstræti

Grundarst

Bus Stop

Hallargarður Park

Bus Stop

Skothúsvegur

Tjarnagata

Bjarkargata

Tjörnin

N

0   200
0   0.1 miles

National Museum

Hljómskálagarður Park

Reykjavík Art Museum – Hafnarhús

Experiences

Reykjavík Art Museum – Hafnarhús
ART MUSEUM

1 ◎ Map p28, C1

Reykjavík Art Museum's Hafnarhús is a marvellously restored warehouse converted into a soaring steel-and-concrete exhibition space. Though the well-curated exhibitions of cutting-edge contemporary Icelandic art change frequently (think installations, videos, paintings and sculpture), you can count on an area with the comic-book-style paintings of Erró (Guðmundur Guðmundsson), a political artist who has donated several thousand works to the museum. The **cafe** has great harbour views. (📞590 1200; www.artmuseum.is; Tryggvagata 17; adult/child Ikr1300/free; ⏱10am-5pm Fri-Wed, to 8pm Thu)

Tjörnin
LAKE

2 ◎ Map p28, B4

This placid lake at the centre of the city is sometimes locally called the Pond. It echoes with the honks and squawks of over 40 species of visiting birds, including swans, geese and Arctic terns; feeding the ducks is a popular pastime for the under-fives. Pretty sculpture-dotted parks like **Hljómskálagarður** line the southern shores, and their paths are much used by cyclists and joggers. In winter, hardy souls strap on ice skates and turn the lake into an **outdoor rink**.

Understand
Icelandic Settlement & Sagas
- -

Rumour, myth and fantastic tales of fierce storms and barbaric dog-headed people kept most explorers away from the great northern ocean, *oceanus innavigabilis*. Irish monks who regularly sailed to the Faroe Islands looking for seclusion were probably the first to stumble upon Iceland. It's thought that they settled around the year 700 but fled when Norsemen began to arrive in the early 9th century.

The Age of Settlement
The Age of Settlement is traditionally defined as between 870 and 930, when political strife on the Scandinavian mainland caused many to flee. Most North Atlantic Norse settlers were ordinary citizens: farmers and merchants who settled across Western Europe, marrying Britons, Westmen (Irish) and Scots.

Among Iceland's first Norse visitors was Norwegian Flóki Vilgerðarson, who uprooted his farm and headed for Snæland around 860. He navigated with ravens, which, after some trial and error, led him to his destination and provided his nickname, Hrafna-Flóki (Raven-Flóki). Hrafna-Flóki sailed to Vatnsfjörður on the west coast but became disenchanted with the conditions. On seeing the icebergs in the fjord he dubbed the country Ísland (Iceland) and returned to Norway. He did eventually settle in Iceland's Skagafjörður district.

According to the 12th-century *Íslendingabók* (a historical narrative of the Settlement Era), Ingólfur Arnarson fled Norway with his blood brother Hjörleifur, landing at Ingólfshöfði (southeast Iceland) in 871. They continued around the coast, and Ingólfur was then led to Reykjavík by a pagan ritual: he tossed his high-seat pillars (a symbol of authority) into the sea as they approached land. Wherever the gods brought the pillars ashore would be the settlers' new home. Ingólfur named Reykjavík (Smoky Bay) after the steam from its thermal springs. Hjörleifur settled near the present town of Vík, but was murdered by his slaves shortly thereafter.

The Saga Age
The late 12th century kicked off the Saga Age, when the epic tales of the earlier 9th-to-10th-century settlement were recorded by historians and writers. These sweeping prose epics or 'sagas' detail the family struggles, romance, vendettas and colourful characters of Settlement, and are the backbone of medieval Icelandic literature, and a rich source for historical understanding (see also the boxed text, p115).

i8
GALLERY

3 ⊙ Map p28, B1

This gallery represents some of the country's top modern artists, many of whom show overseas as well. (☎551 3666; www.i8.is; Tryggvagata 16; admission free; ⏱11am-5pm Tue-Fri, 1-5pm Sat)

Austurvöllur
PARK

4 ⊙ Map p28, C2

Grassy Austurvöllur was once part of first-settler Ingólfur Arnarson's hay fields. Today it's a favourite spot for cafe lounging or lunchtime picnics and summer sunbathing next to the Alþingi; it's also sometimes used for open-air concerts and political demonstrations. The **statue** in the centre is of Jón Sigurðsson, who led the campaign for Icelandic independence.

Alþingi
HISTORIC BUILDING

5 ⊙ Map p28, C2

Iceland's first parliament, the Alþingi, was created at Þingvellir in AD 930. After losing its independence in the 13th century, the country gradually won back its autonomy, and the modern Alþingi moved into this current basalt building in 1881; a stylish glass-and-stone annexe was completed in 2002. Visitors can attend **sessions** (four times weekly October to May; see website for details) when parliament is sitting. (Parliament; www.althingi.is; Kirkjustræti; admission free)

Ráðhús
NOTABLE BUILDING

6 ⊙ Map p28, B3

Reykjavík's waterside Ráðhús is a beautifully positioned postmodern construction of concrete stilts, tinted windows and mossy walls rising from Tjörnin. Inside there's one of the city's top cafe-restaurants, Við Tjörnina (p33), and an interesting 3D map of Iceland. (Vonarstræti; admission free; ⏱8am-7pm Mon-Fri, noon-6pm Sat & Sun)

Reykjavík Museum of Photography
MUSEUM

7 ⊙ Map p28, C1

This gallery room above Reykjavík City Library is worth a visit for its top-notch exhibitions of regional photographers. If you take the lift up, descend by the stairs, which are lined with vintage black-and-white photos. (Ljósmyndasafn Reykjavíkur; ☎411 6390; www.photomuseum.is; Tryggvagata 15, 6th fl, Grófarhús; admission free; ⏱noon-7pm Mon-Thu, to 6pm Fri, 1-5pm Sat & Sun)

Volcano House
FILM

8 ⊙ Map p28, B1

This modern theatre with a lava exhibit in the foyer screens a 55-minute pair of films, in English, about the Westman Island volcanoes and Eyjafjallajökull. They show in German once daily in summer. (☎555 1900; www.volcanohouse.is; Tryggvagata 11; adult/child Ikr1990/500; ⏱hourly 10am-9pm)

Dómkirkja
CHURCH

9 ⊙ Map p28, C3

Iceland's main cathedral, Dómkirkja is a modest affair, but it played a vital role in the country's conversion to Lutheranism. The current building (built in the 18th century and enlarged in 1848) is small and perfectly proportioned, with a plain wooden interior animated by glints of gold. (www.domkirkjan.is; Kirkjustræti; ⊙10am-4.30pm Mon-Fri, mass 11am Sun)

Eating

Nora Magasin
BISTRO €€

10 ✗ Map p28, C2

Hip and open-plan, this buzzy bistro-bar serves up a tasty run of burgers, salads and fresh fish mains creatively conceived by popular chef Völundur Völundarson. Coffee and cocktails run

---

Q **Local Life**

The City's Best Hot Dogs

Icelanders swear the city's best hot dogs are at the **Bæjarins Beztu** (Map p28, D2; www.bbp.is; Tryggvagata; hot dogs Ikr380; ⊙10am-2am Sun-Thu, to 4.30am Fri & Sat; 🖼) truck near the harbour (patronised by Bill Clinton and late-night bar hoppers). Use the vital sentence '*Eina með öllu*' ('One with everything') to get the quintessential favourite with sweet mustard, ketchup and crunchy onions.

---

all night, but the kitchen closes at 10pm or 11pm. (☎578 2010; Pósthússtræti 9; mains Ikr1900-2500; ⊙11.30am-1am Sun-Thu, to 3am Fri & Sat)

Grillmarkaðurinn
FUSION €€€

11 ✗ Map p28, D2

Tippety-top dining is the order of the day here, from the moment you enter the glass atrium with the golden-globe lights to your first snazzy cocktail, and on through the meal. Service is impeccable, and locals and visitors alike rave about the food: locally sourced Icelandic ingredients prepared with culinary imagination by master chefs. (Grill Market; ☎571 7777; www.grillmarkadurinn.is; Lækargata 2a; mains Ikr4200-7200)

Fiskfélagið
INTERNATIONAL €€€

12 ✗ Map p28, C1

The 'Fish Company' takes Icelandic seafood recipes and spins them through a variety of far-flung inspirations from Fiji coconut to Spanish chorizo. Dine in an intimate-feeling stone-and-timber room with copper light fittings and quirky furnishings. (www.fishcompany.is; Vesturgata 2a; mains lunch Ikr1600-2800, dinner Ikr3800-5400; ⊙11.30am-2pm & 6-11.30pm)

Bergsson Mathús
CAFE €

13 ✗ Map p28, C3

This popular, no-nonsense cafe features homemade breads, fresh produce and filling lunch specials.

Alþingi (parliament; p31)

Stop by on weekends when locals flip through magazines, gossip and devour scrumptious brunch plates. (📞571 1822; www.bergsson.is; Templarasund 3; mains Ikr1300-2200; ⏱7am-7pm Mon-Fri, to 5pm Sat & Sun; ✈)

Laundromat Café INTERNATIONAL €€

This popular Danish import – downstairs from high-end cocktail bar Loftið (see 19 🍸 Map p28, C2) – attracts both locals and travellers who devour heaps of hearty mains in a cheery environment surrounded by tattered paperbacks. Go for the 'Dirty Brunch' (Ikr2690) on weekends, to sop up the previous night's booze. Oh, and yes, there are (busy) washers and dryers in the basement (Ikr500/100 per wash/15-minute dry). (www.thelaundromatcafe.com; Austurstræti 9; mains Ikr1000-2700; ⏱8am-midnight Mon-Wed & Sun, to 1am Thu & Fri, 10am-1am Sat; 🛜👶)

Við Tjörnina ICELANDIC €€

14 🍴 Map p28, B3

People are loyal to this well-regarded restaurant – freshly relocated to the city hall, with wraparound windows and lake views – for its beautifully presented Icelandic seafood and other regional dishes like lamb fillet with barley. By day it's a relaxing cafe. (📞551 8666; www.vidtjornina.is; Vonarstræti, Ráðhús; mains Ikr3600-4600; ⏱noon-5pm & 6-10pm)

Icelandic Fish & Chips
ORGANIC, SEAFOOD €€

Pick your fish, and voilà, spelt-batter fried it becomes. Pair it with local beer, organic salads (Ikr750 to Ikr950) and 'Skyronnaises' – *skyr*-based sauces that add a zing to this traditional dish. It's located in the Volcano House (see 8 ◉ Map p28, B1) complex. (☎ 511 1118; www.fishandchips.is; Tryggvagata 11; fish Ikr1450; ⏰ 11.30am-9pm)

Fiskmarkaðurinn
SEAFOOD €€€

15 ✕ Map p28, B2

This restaurant excels in infusing Icelandic seafood and local produce with Far Eastern flavours. For example, the tasting menu (Ikr9900) takes local catches (lobsters from Höfn, salmon from the Þjórsá, halibut from Breiðafjörður) and introduces them to chillis, papaya, coconut and satay glazes. (☎ 578 8877; www.fiskmarkadurinn. is; Aðalstræti 12; mains Ikr4300-6300; ⏰ 11.30am-2pm & 6-11.30pm Mon-Fri, 6-11.30pm Sat & Sun)

Café Paris
INTERNATIONAL €€

16 ✕ Map p28, C2

This is one of the city's prime people-watching spots, particularly in summer when outdoor seating spills onto Austurvöllur square; and at night, when the leather-upholstered interior fills with tunes and tinkling wine glasses. The mediocre selection of sandwiches, salads and burgers is secondary to the

---

Understand
Icelandic Pop

Iceland's pop music scene is one of its great gifts to the world. Internationally famous Icelandic musicians include (of course) Björk and her former band, the Sugarcubes. Sigur Rós followed Björk to stardom; their concert movie *Heima* (2007) is a must-see. Indie-folk Of Monsters and Men stormed the US charts in 2011 with *My Head Is an Animal*. Most lately Ásgeir had a breakout hit with *In the Silence* (2014).

Reykjavík's flourishing music landscape is constantly changing – visit www.icelandmusic.is and www.grapevine.is for news and listings. Just a few examples of local groups include Seabear, an indie-folk band, which spawned top acts like Sin Fang (*Flowers*; 2013) and Sóley (*We Sink*; 2012). Árstíðir record minimalist indie-folk, and had a 2013 viral YouTube hit when they sang a 13th-century Icelandic hymn in a train station. GusGus, a pop-electronica act, opened for Justin Timberlake at his sold-out 2014 Reykjavík concert. Other local bands include FM Belfast (electronica) and múm (experimental electronica mixed with traditional instruments).

If your visit coincides with one of Iceland's many music festivals (p134), go!

scene. (☏551 1020; www.cafeparis.is; Austurstræti 14; mains Ikr2300-5300; ☉8am-1am Sun-Thu, to 2am Fri & Sat; 🛜)

Lobster Hut
SEAFOOD €

17 ❌ Map p28, D2

What's it gonna be? Lobster soup? Lobster salad? Sandwich? This little food truck dishes it all out, for fine diners on the run. If you can't see the truck on Tryggvagata, check down on the corner of Hverfisgata. (cnr Lækergata & Tryggvagata; mains Ikr990-1890; ☉11am-8pm)

Drinking

Micro Bar
BAR

18 🍺 Map p28, C2

Boutique brews is the name of the game at this low-key spot near Austurvöllur. Bottles of beer represent a slew of brands and countries, but more importantly you'll discover 10 local draughts on tap from the island's top microbreweries: the best selection in Reykjavík. The five-beer minisampler costs Ikr2500; happy hour (5pm to 7pm) offers Ikr600 beers. (Austurstræti 6; ☉2pm-midnight Jun-Sep, 4pm-midnight Oct-May)

Loftið
COCKTAIL BAR

19 🍺 Map p28, C2

Loftið is all about high-end cocktails and good living. Dress up to join the fray at this airy upstairs lounge with

a zinc-bar, retro tailor-shop-inspired decor, vintage tiles and a swank crowd. The well booze here is the top-shelf liquor elsewhere, and they bring in jazzy bands on Thursday nights. (☏551 9400; www.loftidbar.is; Austurstræti 9, 2nd fl; ☉2pm-1am Sun-Thu, 4pm-4am Fri & Sat)

Paloma
CLUB

20 🍺 Map p28, C1

One of Reykjavík's best late-night dance clubs, with DJs upstairs laying down electronica and pop, and a pool table in the basement. Find it in the same building as the Dubliner. (Naustin 1-3; ☉club 10pm-4.30am Fri & Sat, basement bar nightly from 8pm)

Hressingarskálinn
PUB

21 🍺 Map p28, D2

Known as Hressó, this large cafe-bar serves a diverse menu until 10pm – everything from porridge to *plokkfiskur*; mains Ikr1700 to Ikr4500) – then at weekends it loses its civilised veneer and concentrates on drinks and dancing. DJs offer pop and rock Thursday through Saturday. (www.hresso.is; Austurstræti 20; ☉9am-1am Sun-Thu, 10am-4.30am Fri & Sat; 🛜)

Lavabarinn
CLUB

22 🍺 Map p28, D2

DJs get this former illegal gentlemen's club pumping with house, R&B, electronica and pop. (Lækjargata 6; ☉5pm-1am Thu, to 4.30am Fri & Sat)

Entertainment

Húrra
LIVE MUSIC

23 ⭐ Map p28, C1

Dark and raw, this large bar opens up its back room to make a concert venue, with live music or DJs most nights. Run by the same folks as Bravó, it's got six beers on tap and happy hour runs till 10pm (beer/wine Ikr500/700). (Tryggvagata 22; ⏲5pm-1am Sun-Thu, to 4.30am Fri & Sat; 📶)

Iðnó Theatre
THEATRE

24 ⭐ Map p28, C3

Icelandic theatre, tending toward the comedic. (📞551 9181; www.idno.is; Vonarstræti 3)

Q Local Life
Kolaportið Flea Market

Held in a huge industrial building by the harbour, the weekend **Kolaportið Flea Market** (Map p28, C1;www.kolaportid.is; Tryggvagata 19; ⏲11am-5pm Sat & Sun) is a Reykjavík institution. Don't expect much from the secondhand clothes and toys, just enjoy the experience. The food section sells traditional eats like *rúgbrauð* (geothermally baked rye bread), *brauðterta* (layered sandwich bread with mayonnaise-based fillings) and *hákarl* (fermented Greenland shark).

Shopping

Kirsuberjatréð
ARTS & CRAFTS

25 🔒 Map p28, B1

This women's art-and-design collective, located in an interesting 1882 former bookstore, sells weird and wonderful fish-skin handbags, music boxes made from string and, our favourite, beautiful coloured bowls made from radish slices. It's been around for 20 years and now has 12 designers. (Cherry Tree; 📞562 8990; www.kirs.is; Vesturgata 4; ⏲10am-7pm Mon-Fri, to 5pm Sat, to 4pm Sun)

Kraum
ARTS & CRAFTS

26 🔒 Map p28, B2

The brainchild of a band of local artists, Kraum literally means 'simmering', like the island's quaking earth and the inventive minds of its citizens. Expect a fascinating assortment of unique designer wares, like fish-skin apparel and driftwood furniture, on display in Reykjavík's oldest house. (www.kraum.is; Aðalstræti 10; ⏲9am-6pm Mon-Fri, noon-5pm Sat & Sun)

Iceland Giftstore
SOUVENIRS

27 🔒 Map p28, D2

If you can see your way past the stuffed puffin in the window, you'll find one of the city's better souvenir shops, with loads of woollens, crafts and collectibles. It also has a Keflavík International Airport location. (Ram-

Café Paris (p34)

magerðin; ☏ 535 6690; www.icelandgiftstore.
com; Hafnarstræti 19; ☺9am-10pm Mon-Fri,
10am-10pm Sat & Sun)

Eymundsson
BOOKS

28 🛍 Map p28, C2

This big central bookshop has a
superb choice of English-language
books, newspapers, magazines and
maps, along with a great cafe. A
second branch can be found on
Skólavörðustígur 11. (www.eymundson.
is; Austurstræti 18; ☺9am-10pm Mon-Fri,
10am-10pm Sat & Sun)

Gaga
CLOTHING

29 🛍 Map p28, C1

Whacky knitted and felt gear from
designer Gaga Skorrdal. (☏551 2306;
www.gaga.is; Vesturgata 4; ☺10am-6pm
Mon-Fri, to 4pm Sat)

Kickstart
CLOTHING

30 🛍 Map p28, B1

This tiny but inviting men's store
stocks ties, gloves, motorcycle gear
and other manly accoutrements.
(☏568 0809; www.kickstart.is; Vesturgata 12;
☺10am-5.30pm Mon-Fri)

Explore

Old Harbour

Largely a service harbour until recently, the Old Harbour has blossomed into a hot spot for tourists, with several museums, volcano and Northern Lights films, and interesting eateries. Whale-watching and puffin-viewing trips depart from the pier, and, as boat bells ding, photo ops abound with views of the Harpa concert hall and snowcapped mountains beyond.

Experiences in a Day

Start your day with a **whale-watching trip** (p40) from the Old Harbour, cruising nearby waters in search of cetaceans, seabirds and open skies. Then have lunch at one of the area's good, casual restaurants, from the **Walk the Plank** (p45) crab slider trolley to rustic but excellent seafood joint **Sægreifinn** (p44) or hamburger hang-out **Hamborgara Búllan** (p47).

Grab a coffee at **Café Haiti** (p47) before heading on to the museum of your choice: **Víkin Maritime Museum** (p43) for nautical history, the **Saga Museum** (p43) for bloodthirsty Saga simulations, **Aurora Reykjavík** (p44) for a recreation of the grand borealis or **Whales of Iceland** (p44) for life-size reconstructions of the great beasts you spotted in the morning. The **Cinema at Old Harbour Village No 2** (p44) is perfect for catching Icelandic nature films about volcanoes and the Northern Lights. An ice cream at **Valdi's** (p44) will give you a second wind.

Wrap up your evening early with dinner at **Forréttabarinn** (p44) and cocktails across the street at chic **Slippbarinn** (p47).

◉ Top Experiences

Whale Watching (p40)

♥ Best of Reykjavík

Cafes & Bars
Café Haiti (p47)

Slippbarinn (p47)

With Kids
Whale Watching (p40)

Whales of Iceland (p44)

Saga Museum (p43)

Aurora Reykjavík (p44)

Valdi's (p44)

Getting There

🚍 **Bus** Bus 14 runs all the way across town: from Kringlan shopping centre to Laugardalur park to Hlemmur bus station, the National Museum, Old Reykjavík and finally the Old Harbour. The Mýrargata stop is nearest for the whale-watching outfits and several restaurants, while Grandagarður is closest to the Víkin Maritime Museum and other sights.

Top Experiences
Whale Watching

Whale watching is one of Iceland's most beloved pastimes, and boats depart year-round to catch glimpses of these magnificent beasts as they wave their fins, spout and dive. Northern waters around Húsavík and Akureyri are famous, but Reykjavík visitors can hop a boat directly from the capital's Old Harbour. From here you'll cruise the frigid waters in search of minke, humpback and fin whales, though an occasional orca (killer whale) or even blue whale may be spotted. Trips are also tops for birdwatching.

◉ Map p42, D3

Old Harbour, north of Mýrargata

Don't Miss

Whales

The most common whales you'll spot on boats from Reykjavík are humpback whales and minke whales. The humpback is known for its curious nature and spectacular surface displays. The minke has a stream-lined, slender black body, a white-striped pectoral fin and a tendency to leap entirely out of the water.

Porpoises & Dolphins

Keep an eye out for tiny, shy harbour porpoises (*Phocoena phocoena*), which are easiest to spot in placid conditions. More gregarious white-beaked dolphins (*Lagenorhynchus albirostris*) often travel in larger pods, approach and accompany the boats, and can also be found in winter.

Puffins & Seabirds

The bird life in Iceland is abundant, especially during the warmest months when migrating species arrive to nest. You may see Arctic terns, gannets, guillemots and kittiwakes, among many more, but the stars of the show are the zippy, cutesy puffins.

Tour Operators

▶ **Elding Adventures at Sea** (☑519 5000; www.whale-watching.is; Ægisgarður 5; ☼harbour kiosk 8am-9pm) The most established and ecofriendly outfit. Includes whale exhibition, angling and puffin-watching trips, as well as combo tours. Also runs the ferry to Viðey.

▶ **Special Tours** (☑560 8800; www.specialtours.is; Ægisgarður 13; ☼harbour kiosk 8am-8pm) Small, fast boat used for sea angling and whale watching. Also puffin and combo tours.

▶ **Sea Safari** (☑861 3840; www.seasafari.is; Ægisgarður 9) Offers whale-watching (1½ hours; Ikr15,000) and puffin tours (one hour; Ikr 5000) in a Zodiac.

☑ Top Tips

▶ Tour ticket prices start at around Ikr8500 for a two- to three-hour trip; Ikr4250 for kids.

▶ Tours generally run year-round with more departures in May to August (prime viewing season).

▶ If you don't spot whales, many outfitters offer vouchers to come back and try again.

▶ Several companies also offer sea-angling (adult/child from Ikr11,500/5750) and puffin-viewing trips (from Ikr5000/2500), though you'll often see puffins while whale watching.

▶ Trips are cancelled when sea conditions are foul.

✗ Take a Break

The closest spot to grab a bite is crab-sandwich trolley, Walk the Plank (p45), which sets up on the pier during whale-watching season.

Otherwise, hit Hamborgara Búllan (p47) for burgers, Sægreifinn (p44) for fish or Café Haiti (p47) for top coffee.

Old Harbour

For reviews see
◉ Top Experiences   p40
◎ Experiences   p43
✖ Eating   p44
🍷 Drinking   p47
🛍 Shopping   p47

100 m
0.05 miles

Old Harbour

ÖRFIRISEY

Whales of Iceland ◉ 3

Bus Stop

Frakkastíð

Víkin Maritime Museum ◉ 1

✖ 9   Grandagarður

Saga Museum ◎ 2

Aurora Reykjavík ◎ 4

Bus Stop

Boardwalk

Walking Area/Wharf

Whale Watching ◉

Ægisgarður

✖ 8

Cinema at Old Harbour Village No 2
◎ 2
✖ 6 ◎ 5
◉ 12 13
✖ 10

Ýsisgata

11 🍷

Mýrargata

Bus Stop ✖ 7

Nylendugata

Bakkastígur

Vesturgata

Seljavegur

Vesturgata

Ránargata

Recreation of the Battle of Orlygsstathir, Saga Museum

Experiences

Víkin Maritime Museum MUSEUM

1 ◉ Map p42, B2

Based appropriately in a former fish-freezing plant, this small museum celebrates the country's seafaring heritage, focusing on the trawlers that transformed Iceland's economy. Your ticket also allows you aboard coastguard ship *Óðinn* by guided tour (11am, 1pm, 2pm and 3pm, reduced hours during winter, closed January and February). The boat is a veteran of the 1970s Cod Wars, when British and Icelandic fishermen came to blows over fishing rights in the North Atlantic. (Víkin Sjóminjasafnið; ☏517 9400; www.sjominjasafn.is; Grandagarður 8; adult/child Ikr1200/free; ⊙10am-5pm Jun–mid-Sep, 11am-5pm Tue-Sun mid-Sep–May)

Saga Museum MUSEUM

2 ◉ Map p42, A3

The endearingly bloodthirsty Saga Museum is where Icelandic history is brought to life by eerie silicon models and a multilingual soundtrack with thudding axes and hair-raising screams. Don't be surprised if you see some of the characters wandering around town, as moulds were taken from Reykjavík residents (the owner's daughters are the Irish princess and the little slave gnawing a fish!). (☏511 1517; www.sagamuseum.is; Grandagarður 2; adult/child Ikr2000/800; ⊙9am-6pm)

Local Life
Ice Cream!

Happy families flock to iconic **Valdi's** (Map p42, C1; ☎ 586 8088; www.valdis.is; Grandagarður 21; scoop Ikr425; ⏱ 11.30am-11pm May-Aug; ♿) throughout summer. Take a number and join the crush waiting to choose a scoop from the huge array of homemade ice creams. It's totally casual, and totally fun.

Whales of Iceland   MUSEUM

3 ◉ Map p42, A1

Ever stroll beneath a blue whale? This brand-new museum houses full-sized models of the 23 whales found off Iceland's coast. The largest museum of this type in Europe, it also displays models of whale skeletons and has a cafe and gift shop. (☎ 571 0077; www. whalesoficeland.com; Fiskislóð 23-25; adult/ child Ikr2800/1550; ⏱ 10am-7pm May-Sep, to 6pm Oct-Apr)

Aurora Reykjavík   EXHIBITION

4 ◉ Map p42, B3

Learn about the classical tales explaining the Northern Lights, and the scientific explanation, then watch a 35-minute surround-sound panoramic HD recreation of Icelandic auroras. (Northern Lights Centre; ☎ 780 4500; www.aurorareykjavik.is; Grandagarður 2; adult/child Ikr1600/1000; ⏱ 9am-9pm)

Cinema at Old Harbour Village No 2   FILM

5 ◉ Map p42, D4

A tiny theatre perches in the top of one of the rehabbed Old Harbour warehouses. Nature films include volcanoes (Hekla, Eyjafjallajökull, Westmann Islands), the creation of Iceland, þingvellir and the Northern Lights, and are mostly shown in English with occasional German screenings. See schedule online. (☎ 899 7953; www.thecinema.is; Geirsgata 7b; adult/child Ikr1500/750)

Eating

Sægreifinn   SEAFOOD €

6 🍴 Map p42, D4

Sidle into this green harbour-side shack for the most famous lobster soup (Ikr1300) in the capital, or to choose from a fridge full of fresh fish skewers to be grilled on the spot. Though the original sea baron sold the restaurant a few years ago, the place retains a homey, laid-back feel. (Seabaron; ☎ 553 1500; www.saegreifinn.is; Geirsgata 8; mains Ikr1350-1900; ⏱ 11.30am-11pm)

Forréttabarinn   TAPAS €€

7 🍴 Map p42, C4

Tapas restaurants are popular in the capital, and this hip joint near the harbour is a favourite for its new menu of creative plates like cod and pork belly with celery root purée. There is also an airy and relaxed bar area, with weathered wood tables and broad couches. (Starter Bar; ☎ 517 1800; www.forrettabarinn. is; Nýlendugata 14, entrance from Mýrargata; plates Ikr1480-2250; ☺11.30am-10pm Sun-Wed, to midnight Thu-Sat)

Walk the Plank   SEAFOOD €

8 🍴 Map p42, D3

On decent-weather days and around whale-watching departures, this tiny food truck opens its window and dishes up yummy crab-cake sliders on the quay. (Ægisgarður; mains Ikr1500-1900; ☺10am-8pm)

Coocoo's Nest   CAFE €€

9 🍴 Map p42, C2

Pop into this cool eatery tucked behind the Old Harbour for popular weekend brunches (11am to 4pm) paired with decadent cocktails (Ikr1800). Casual, small and groovy,

---

Understand
Eating the Locals

Many restaurants and tour operators in Iceland tout their more unusual delicacies: whale (*hvál/hvalur*), fermented shark (*hákarl*) and puffin (*lundi*). Before you dig in, consider that what may have been sustainable for 325,000 Icelanders becomes taxing on species and delicate ecosystems when one million tourists per year get involved.

▶ 35% to 40% of Icelandic whale meat consumption is by tourists.

▶ 75% of Icelanders do not buy whale meat.

▶ 80% of the minke whale is thrown away after killing.

▶ Fin whales are classified as Endangered.

▶ Iceland's Ministry of Industries and Innovation maintains the whale catch is sustainable, at less than 1% of local stock, despite international protest.

▶ The Greenland shark, which is used for *hákarl,* has a conservation status of Near Threatened.

▶ In 2003 there were an estimated eight million puffins in Iceland; in 2014 there were about five million – a 37% drop.

▶ At the time of research, Icelandic puffins were experiencing an enormous breeding failure in their largest colonies, in the Vestmannaeyja.

▶ Find whale-free eateries at http://icewhale.is/whale-friendly-restaurants.

Understand
Partying in Reykjavík

Reykjavík's renowned *djammið*, should not be confused with the coun-tryside *rúntur*, which involves Icelandic youth driving around their town in one big automotive party. For a tamer version of *djammið* you could say *pöbbarölt* meaning 'pub stroll'.

The action is concentrated near Laugavegur and Austurstræti. Places stay open until 1am Sunday to Thursday (4am or 5am on Friday and Saturday). You'll pay Ikr800 to Ikr1200 per pint of beer, and cocktails are Ikr1800 to Ikr2600. Some venues have cover charges (about Ikr1000) after midnight; many have early happy hours saving Ikr500 to Ikr700 per beer. Download smartphone *Reykjavík Appy Hour* app, and check **Grapevine** (www.grapevine.is) for latest listings.

Thanks to the high price of alcohol, things generally don't get going until late. Icelanders brave the melee at government alcohol store **Vín-búðin** (www.vinbudin.is; Austurstræti 10a; ⊙11am-6pm Mon-Thu & Sat, to 7pm Fri), then toddle home for a prepub party.

Local Liquors

Check out **Brennivín** (http://brennivin.is), a neon-green, caraway-flavoured 'black death' schnapps; **Opal** a flavoured vodka in several menthol and liquorice varieties; **Flóki Whisky** (www.flokiwhisky.is), an Icelandic single malt whisky; the **64° Reykjavík Distillery** (www.reykjavikdistillery.is), a micro-distillery producing Katla vodka, aquavit, herbal liqueurs and schnapps; and **Reyka Vodka** (www.reyka.com), Iceland's first distillery, in Borgarnes.

Beer!

Egils, Gull, Thule and Viking are the most common beers (typically lagers) in Iceland. But craft breweries are taking the scene by storm. Try **Borg Brugghús** (www.borgbrugghus.is), an award-winning craft brew-ery with scrumptious beers from Brío pilsner to Garún stout; **Einstök Brewing Company** (www.einstokbeer.com), an Akureyri-based craft brew-ery with a distinctive Icelandic Pale Ale, among other ales and porters; **Bruggsmiðjan–Kaldi** (www.bruggsmidjan.is), produced using Czech tech-niques; **Steðji Brugghús** (www.stedji.com), a brewhouse offering lager and seasonal beers; and **Ölvisholt Brugghús** (www.brugghus.is) with micro-brews from south Iceland, including eye-catching Lava beer.

with mozaic plywood tables. The menu changes, but it's always scrumptious. (Grandagarður 23; mains Ikr1500-2700; ⊘11am-7pm Tue-Fri, to 10pm Sat, to 4pm Sun; 🛜)

Víkin Cafe CAFE €

The on-site cafe of the Víkin Maritime Museum (see 1 ◉ Map p42, B2) offers relaxing views of the boat-filled harbour and has a great sunny-weather terrace. (Grandagarður 8; snacks Ikr800-1890; 10am-5pm Jun–mid-Sep, 11am-5pm Tue-Sun mid-Sep–May)

Hamborgara Búllan FAST FOOD €

10 ✖ Map p42, C4

The Old Harbour's outpost of burgerdom and Americana proffers savoury patties that are perennial local favourites. Russell Crowe was spotted here while filming in 2012. (Hamborgarabúlla Tómasar; 📞511 1888; www.bullan.is; Geirsgata 1; mains Ikr730-1400; ⊘11.30am-9pm; 👶)

Drinking

Slippbarinn COCKTAIL BAR

11 🍷 Map p42, C4

Jetsetters unite at this buzzy hotel, restaurant and bar at the Old Harbour. It's bedecked with vintage record players and chatting locals sipping some of the best cocktails in town. (📞560 8080; www.slippbarinn.is; Mýrargata 2; ⊘11.30am-midnight Sun-Thu, to 1am Fri & Sat)

Café Haiti CAFE

12 🍷 Map p42, D4

If you're a coffee aficionado, this tiny cafe in the Old Harbour is the place for you. Owner Elda buys her beans from her home country Haiti, and roasts and grinds them on-site, producing what regulars swear are the best cups of coffee in the country. (📞588 8484; www.cafehaiti.is; Geirsgata 7c; ⊘8am-10pm Mon-Thu, to 11pm Fri, 9am-11pm Sat, to 10pm Sun)

Shopping

Fabúla ARTS & CRAFTS

13 🔒 Map p42, D4

Whacky-wonderful statuettes, ceramics and paintings brighten up an old warehouse in the Old Harbour. It also offers a few items by Icelandic clothing and jewellery designers. (📞555 2503; Geirsgata 7; ⊘11am-6pm Mon-Fri, to 4pm Sat)

Explore

Laugavegur & Skólavörðustígur

Reykjavík's main street for shopping and people-watching is bustling, often-pedestrianised Laugavegur. The narrow, one-way lane and its side streets blossom with the capital's most interesting shops, cafes and bars. At its western end, its name changes to Bankastræti, then Austurstræti. Running uphill off Bankastræti, artists' street Skólavörðustígur ends at spectacular modernist church, Hallgrímskirkja.

Experiences in a Day

☀️ Breakfast at **Grái Kötturinn** (p58) then be dazzled by the shiny surfaces and gorgeous interior of **Harpa** (p55), before choosing among the neighbourhood's many museums. Hit the **Icelandic Phallological Museum** (p55) to see coolly curated penises before perusing top art at the **Reykjavík Art Museum – Kjarvalsstaðir** (p55) or at either of the (other) Jónsson museums: **Ásgrímur Jónsson Collection** (p56) or **Einar Jónsson Museum** (p56).

☀️ Get a bite to eat at delicious, organic **Gló** (p58), then zip to the top of **Hallgrímskirkja** (p50) for views. If you're up for more art, head over to the excellent, small **National Gallery of Iceland** (p55), by the lake. If you'd rather unwind, take a dip in the geothermal pools at the classic **Sundhöllin** (p57).

🌙 Be sure to reserve ahead for any of the area's top restaurants, which are some of the best in the country: **Dill** (p57), **Snaps** (p58) or **Þrír Frakkar** (p58). Or kick off a late-night *djammið* party blow-out with casual eats at lively **K-Bar** (p58) or **KEX** (p60). Quieter night? Take in an Icelandic flick at **Bíó Paradís** (p62).

For a local's night out on the town, see p52.

👁️ Top Experiences
Hallgrímskirkja (p50)

🔍 Local Life
Djammið Nightlife (p52)

💜 Best of Reykjavík

Eating
Dill (p57)

Þrír Frakkar (p58)

Gló (p58)

Ostabúðin (p59)

Grái Kötturinn (p58)

Shopping
Kiosk (p63)

KronKron (p63)

Handknitting Association of Iceland (p63)

Leynibúðin (p64)

Getting There

🚶 On Foot Within the neighbourhood it's easiest to walk, as many of the roads are one-way or pedestrianised.

🚌 Bus Buses 1, 3, 6, 11, 12 and 13 run between the Hlemmur bus terminal at the eastern end of Laugavegur, along the waterfront to Lækjartorg Square (the city's other bus terminal), before continuing onward.

Top Experiences
Hallgrímskirkja

Reykjavík's soaring white-concrete church, star of a thousand postcards, dominates the city skyline, and is visible from 20km away. The graceful church was named after poet Reverend Hallgrímur Pétursson (1614–74), who wrote Iceland's most popular hymn book, *Passion Hymns*. The church's size and radical design caused controversy, and its architect, Guðjón Samúelsson (1887–1950), never saw its completion – it took 41 years (1945–86) to build. The church offers great photo ops and thrilling views from its dizzying tower.

👁 Map p54, C4

📞 510 1000

www.hallgrimskirkja.is

Skólavörðustígur

tower adult/child Ikr700/100

🕙9am-9pm Jul & Aug, to 5pm Sep-Jun

Don't Miss

Facade & Tower
The columns on either side of the church's signature 74.5m-high tower represent volcanic basalt, part of architect Guðjón Samúelsson's desire to create a national architectural style. Get a spectacular panorama of the city by taking an elevator trip up the tower to the viewing area.

Organ
In contrast to the high drama outside, the Lutheran church's interior is quite plain. The most eye-catching feature is the vast, gleaming 5275-pipe organ, installed in 1992. It was made in Germany by Johannes Klais Orgelbau and individuals sponsored each of the pipes; their names are inscribed on them. Towards the altar, you'll find the quaint older organ, still in use, too.

Concerts & Services
From mid-June to mid-August, hear **choral concerts** (www.scholacantorum.is) at noon on Wednesdays (admission Ikr2000), and **organ recitals** (www.listvinafelag.is) at noon on Saturdays and some Thursdays (admission Ikr1700) and on Sundays at 5pm (admission Ikr2500). **Services** are held on Sundays at 11am, with small services on Wednesdays at 8am. There is an English service the last Sunday of the month at 2pm.

Leifur Eiríksson Statue
Out front, gazing proudly into the distance is a statue of the Viking Leifur Eiríksson, the first European to discover America. A present from the USA on the 1000th anniversary of the Alþingi (parliament) in 1930, it was designed by Alexander Stirling Calder (1870–1945), the father of the perhaps more famous, modern mobilist and sculptor Alexander Calder (1898–1976).

☑ Top Tips

▶ Try for a local's pronunciation: Hallgrímskirkja is pronounced hatl-krims-kirk-ya.

▶ There are occasional rotating art exhibitions in the church's foyer.

▶ Check online for the schedule of organ and choral recitals during your visit.

✗ Take a Break

In fair weather a sweet little soup wagon, Soup Car (p60), sets up near the plaza in front of the church and serves up bowls of lamb stew or vegan soup. Or head down Skólavörðustígur to a plethora of eateries; try the classic Kaffi Mokka (p61), one of Reykjavík's first coffee shops, for a light meal.

Local Life
Djammið Nightlife

Reykjavík is renowned for its wild, wonderful party scene. Called *djammið* (meaning going out on the town), the high-spirited nightlife is at its roaringest on weekends: many cafes and bistros transform into raucous beer-soaked bars, joining the dedicated pubs and clubs. But it's not the quantity of drinking dens that makes Reykjavík's nightlife special – it's the crowd's upbeat energy.

1 **Warming Up**

As any good pub crawler knows, you gotta warm up so you don't break something. Start the night at **Kaldi** (www.kaldibar.is; Laugavegur 20b; ☺noon-1am Sun-Thu, to 3am Fri & Sat) while you're still in the mood to discern quality beer. Effortlessly cool with mismatched seats and teal banquettes, plus a popular smoking courtyard, Kaldi carries the full range of its own

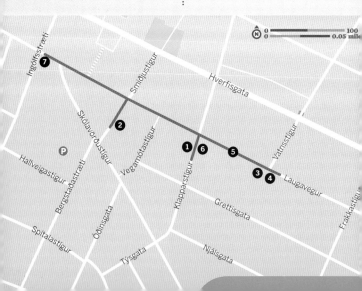

microbrews, not available elsewhere. Anyone can play the piano.

❷ The Beautiful People

The old house with the London Underground symbol over the door contains one of Reykjavík's coolest bars: **Kaffibarinn** (www.kaffibarinn.is; Bergstaðastræti 1; ⊙2pm-1am Sun-Thu, to 4.30am Fri & Sat). It had a starring role in the cult movie *101 Reykjavík* (2000), and at weekends you may need a famous face or a battering ram to get in, it's so packed.

❸ Cool Cats

If you couldn't get into Kaffibarinn, or you're just ready to move on, head down to cool, arty **Boston** (☎577 3200; Laugavegur 28b; ⊙4pm-1am Sun-Thu, to 3am Fri & Sat). You'll find it up through a doorway on Laugavegur that leads to this laid-back lounge where hip locals hang, and where DJs spin from time to time.

❹ Rock Out!

Or, go next door for beer, beards and the odd flying bottle...atmospheric **Dillon** (☎578 2424; Laugavegur 30; ⊙2pm-1am Sun-Thu, to 3am Fri & Sat) is a RRRROCK pub with a great beer garden. Frequent concerts hit its tiny corner stage. Get dark and get sweaty.

❺ The Shank of the Evening

By now you should be feeling the *djammið* vibe; it's a perfect time to simply stroll packed Laugavegur, people-watching and striking up conversations. This may be the moment where you toss guidebook routes and just roll with the locals: pubs and late-night dives abound throughout the centre.

❻ Time to Dance

Ostensibly a queer bar, **Kiki** (www.kiki. is; Laugavegur 22; ⊙11pm-4.30am Fri & Sat) is also the place to go get your dance on, since much of Reykjavík's nightlife centres around the booze, not the groove. It's only open on weekends, but if you can squeeze beneath the flamingo sign and beyond the rainbow-striped tin siding, you'll find one of Reykjavík's best dance parties.

❼ Staggering Home

The atmosphere at one of Reykjavík's oldest joints, **Prikið** (☎551 2866; www. prikid.is; Bankastræti 12; ⊙8am-1am Mon-Thu, to 4.30am Fri, 11am-4.30am Sat, 11am-1am Sun), falls somewhere between diner and saloon, though it can also get dancey in the wee hours. If you're still standing and you're longing for some greasy eats before heading home, join the locals tucking into burgers or the popular next-day 'hangover killer' breakfast. Or grab a great freshly made pizza slice at **The Deli** (www.deli.is; Bankastræti 14; slices Ikr400; ⊙10am-10pm Mon-Wed, to 2am Thu, to 7am Fri & Sat), just up the block.

For reviews see
- Top Experiences   p50
- Experiences   p55
- Eating   p57
- Drinking   p60
- Entertainment   p62
- Shopping   p63

200 m
0.1 miles

Experiences

Harpa
CULTURAL BUILDING

1 ⊙ Map p54, B1

With its ever-changing facets glistening on the water's edge, Reykjavík's Harpa concert hall and cultural centre is a beauty to behold. In addition to a season of top-notch shows (some free), it's worth stopping by to explore the shimmering interior with harbour vistas or take a 45-minute **tour** (Ikr1500; h9am, 11am, 1.30pm & 3.30pm daily Jun-Aug, 3.30pm Mon-Fri, 11am & 3.30pm Sat and Sun Sep-May) of the hall. (✆ box office 528 5050; www.harpa.is; Austurbakki 2; ⊙ box office 9am-6pm Mon-Fri, 10am-6pm Sat & Sun)

Reykjavík Art Museum – Kjarvalsstaðir
ART MUSEUM

2 ⊙ Map p54, E4

The angular glass-and-wood Kjarvalsstaðir, which looks out onto **Miklatún Park**, is named for Jóhannes Kjarval (1885–1972), one of Iceland's most popular classical artists. He was a fisherman until his crew paid for him to study at the Academy of Fine Arts in Copenhagen, and his wonderfully evocative landscapes share space alongside changing installations of mostly Icelandic 20th-century paintings. (✆517 1290; www.artmuseum.is; Flókagata, Miklatún Park; adult/child Ikr1300/free; ⊙10am-5pm)

Top Tip

Three for the Price of One

▶ The Reykjavík Art Museum ticket covers all three of its sites.

▶ The National Gallery ticket is also good at the nearby Ásgrímur Jónsson Collection, and further-afield Sigurjón Ólafsson Museum (p67).

National Gallery of Iceland
GALLERY

3 ⊙ Map p54, A3

This pretty stack of marble atriums and spacious galleries overlooking Tjörnin offers ever-changing exhibits drawn from the 10,000-piece collection. The museum can only exhibit a small sample at any time; shows range from 19th- and 20th-century paintings by Iceland's favourite sons and daughters (including Jóhannes Kjarval and Nína Sæmundsson) to sculptures by Sigurjón Ólafsson and others. The museum ticket also covers entry to the Ásgrímur Jónsson Collection (p56) and Sigurjón Ólafsson Museum (p67). (Listasafn Íslands; www.listasafn.is; Fríkirkjuvegur 7; adult/child Ikr1000/free; ⊙10am-5pm Tue-Sun Jun-Aug, from 11am Sep-May)

Icelandic Phallological Museum
MUSEUM

4 ⊙ Map p54, E4

Oh, the jokes are endless here, but though this unique museum houses a huge collection of penises, it's actually very well done. From pickled pickles to petrified wood, there are 283 different members on display, representing all Icelandic mammals and beyond. Featured items include contributions from sperm whales and a polar bear, minuscule mouse bits, silver castings of each member of the Icelandic handball team and a single human sample – from deceased mountaineer Páll Arason. (Hið Íslenzka Reðasafn; ☎561 6663; www.phallus.is; Laugavegur 116; adult/child Ikr1250/free; ☺10am-6pm)

Kling & Bang
GALLERY

5 ◉ Map p54, C2

This cutting-edge young artists' exhibition space is a favourite with locals. (☎696 2209; www.this.is/klingobang; Hverfisgata 42; admission free; ☺2-6pm Thu-Sun)

☑ Top Tip

Donating to the Icelandic Phallological Museum

The acquisition of Páll Arason's 'specimen' by the Icelandic Phallological Museum (p55) was the subject of the oddball documentary, *The Final Member* (2012). Five other donors-in-waiting have already promised to bequeath their manhood (signed contracts are mounted on the wall). Interested? Get in line.

Ásgrímur Jónsson Collection
ART MUSEUM

6 ◉ Map p54, A4

Iceland's first professional painter, Ásgrímur Jónsson (1876–1958), was the son of a farmer. He lived and worked here, and you can visit his former atelier to see his work incorporating folk tales and Icelandic nature. (☎515 9625; www.listasafn.is; Bergstaðastræti 74; adult/child Ikr1000/free; ☺2-5pm Tue, Thu & Sun mid-May–mid-Sep, 2-5pm Sun mid-Sep–Nov & Feb–mid-May)

Einar Jónsson Museum
ART MUSEUM

7 ◉ Map p54, C4

Einar Jónsson (1874–1954) is one of Iceland's foremost sculptors, famous for intense symbolist works. Chiselled representations of Hope, Earth and Death burst from basalt cliffs, weep over naked women and slay dragons. Jónsson designed the building, which was built between 1916 and 1923, when this empty hill was the outskirts of town. It also contains his austere penthouse flat and studio, with views over the city. The **sculpture garden** (Freyjugata; admission free) behind the museum contains 26 bronzes, in the shadow of Hallgrímskirkja. (☎561 3797; www.lej.is; Eriksgata; adult/child Ikr1000/free; ☺1-5pm Tue-Sun Jun–mid-Sep, 1-5pm Sat & Sun mid-Sep–Nov & Feb-May)

Culture House

ART MUSEUM

8 Map p54, B2

At the time of writing, this museum was being reimagined as a collaboration between the National Museum, National Gallery and four other organisations as a study of the artistic heritage of Iceland from Settlement to today. Slated to open by early 2015. (Þjóðmenningarhúsið; www.thjodminjasafn.is; Hverfisgata 15; adult/child Ikr1000/free; ⊙11am-5pm)

Sundhöllin

GEOTHERMAL POOL, HOT-POT

9 Map p54, D4

Reykjavík's oldest swimming pool (1937), designed in art-deco style by architect Guðjón Samúelsson, is smack in the centre and offers the only indoor pool within the city, plus Hallgrímskirkja views from the decks. (✆411 5350; Barónsstígur 16; ⊙6.30am-10pm Mon-Thu, to 8pm Fri, 8am-4pm Sat, 10am-6pm Sun; 👪)

Volcano Show

FILM

10 Map p54, A4

Eccentric eruption-chaser Villi Knudsen is the cinematographer and presenter of this film show in a little theatre in an outbuilding on a residential street (not to be confused with Volcano House, p31). Some are captivated by Villi and his films about 50 years of Icelandic volcanoes (eg images of the town of Heimaey being crushed by molten lava), although some footage is a bit old and wobbly, so it's not for everyone. (Red Rock Cinema; ✆845 9548; Hellusund 6a; admission Ikr1500; ⊙twice daily)

Local Life
Design, Art & Craft

Inspired by the amazing local art and design shops? Get involved with graphic design, cooking, arts, crafts, music...you name it! **Creative Iceland** (www.creativeiceland.is) hooks you up with local creative people offering workshops in their art or craft. If you're a knitter, the half-day knitting workshops at **Icelandic Culture and Craft Workshops** (✆566 8822; www.cultureandcraft.com; courses from Isk11,900) use Icelandic wool. **Iceland Design Centre** (Hönnunarmiðstöð; ✆771 2200; www.icelanddesign.is; Vonar-stræti 4b) lists more artists, designers and special events.

Sun-Craft

MONUMENT

11 Map p54, D2

Reykjavík is littered with fascinating sculptures, but it's Jón Gunnar Árnason's ship-like *Sun-Craft* sculpture that seems to catch visitors' imaginations. Scooping in a skeletal arc along the seaside, it offers a photo op with snowcapped mountains in the distance. (Sæbraut)

Eating

Dill

SCANDINAVIAN €€€

12 Map p54, B2

Top 'New Nordic' cuisine is the major drawcard at this elegant yet simple bistro. The focus is very much on the

Local Life
Brunch with Björk

Blink and you'll miss **Grái Köt-turinn** (Map p54, B2; 551 1544; Hverfisgata 16a; mains Ikr1000-2500; 7.15am-3pm Mon-Fri, 8am-3pm Sat & Sun), a tiny six-table cafe (a favour-ite of Björk's). It looks like a cross between an eccentric bookshop and an art gallery, and serves deli-cious breakfasts of toast, bagels, pancakes, or bacon and eggs served on thick, buttery slabs of freshly baked bread.

food – locally sourced produce served as a parade of courses. The owners are friends with the famous Noma clan, and have drawn much inspiration from the celebrated Copenhagen restaurant. Popular with locals and visitors alike, a reservation is a must. (552 1522; www. dillrestaurant.is; Hverfisgata 12; 3-course meal from Ikr8100; 7-10pm Wed-Sat)

Gló   ORGANIC, VEGETARIAN €

Join the cool cats in this upstairs, airy restaurant, next to the Lebowski Bar (see 27 Map p54, B3) serving fresh, large daily specials loaded with Asian-influenced herbs and spices. Though not exclusively vegetarian, it's a wonderland of raw and organic foods with your choice from a broad bar of elaborate salads, from root veggies to Greek. It also has branches in Lau-gardalur and Hafnarfjörður. (553 1111; www.glo.is; Laugavegur 20b; mains Ikr1700-2500; 11am-9pm;)

Snaps   FRENCH €€

13 Map p54, B3

Reserve ahead for this French bistro that's a mega-hit with locals. Snaps' secret is simple: serve scrumptious seafood and classic bistro mains (think steak or mussels and fries) at surprisingly decent prices. Lunch specials (11.30am to 2pm; Ikr1890) and scrummy brunches (11.30am to 4pm Saturday and Sunday; Ikr900 to Ikr3300) are a big draw, too. Seats fill a lively glassed-in porch and have views of the open kitchen. (511 6677; www2.snaps. is; Þórsgata 1; dinner mains Ikr3000-4000; 11.30am-11pm Sun-Thu, to midnight Fri & Sat)

K-Bar   FUSION €€

14 Map p54, D3

Leather banquettes and hammered copper tables at this cool bar-restaurant fill up with lively locals thrilled to dig into creative California-Korean style cuisine from tempura cod sliders to BBQ beef. Cocktails are delish, too, as are local tap beers (Ikr950 to Ikr1400). Brunchy foods like eggs Benedict (Ikr1890) are served till 4pm. (571 6666; Laugavegur 74; mains lunch Ikr1600-1800, dinner Ikr2000-3000; 7.30am-10pm Sun-Thu, to 11.30pm Fri & Sat)

Þrír Frakkar   ICELANDIC, SEAFOOD €€

15 Map p54, B4

Owner-chef Úlfar Eysteinsson has built up a consistently excellent reputation at this snug little restaurant – appar-ently a favourite of Jamie Oliver's. Spe-cialities range throughout the aquatic world from salt cod and halibut to *plokkfiskur* (fish stew) with black bread. Non-fish items run toward guillemot, horse, lamb and whale. (☎552 3939; www.3frakkar.com; Baldursgata 14; mains Ikr3200-5300; ⏱11.30am-2.30pm & 6-11.30pm Mon-Fri, 6-11.30pm Sat & Sun)

Bakarí Sandholt
BAKERY €

Reykjavík's favourite bakery (see **43** 🔒 Map p54, C3) is usually crammed with folks hoovering up the generous assortment of fresh baguettes, croissants, pastries and sandwiches. The soup of the day (Ikr1300) comes with delicious sourdough bread. (☎551 3524; www.sandholt.is; Laugavegur 36; mains Ikr250-980; ⏱6.30am-9pm)

Vegamót
INTERNATIONAL €€

16 ✖ Map p54, B3

A long-running bistro-bar-club, with a name that means 'crossroads', this is still a trendy place to eat, drink, see and be seen at night (it's favoured by families during the day). The 'global' menu ranges all over: from Mexican salad to Louisiana chicken. Weekend brunches (Ikr2000 to Ikr2500) are a hit, too. (☎511 3040; www.vegamot.is; Vegamótastígur 4; mains Ikr2400-4000; ⏱11.30am-1am Mon-Thu, 11am-4am Fri & Sat, noon-1am Sun; 🛜)

Kolabrautin
ITALIAN €€

17 ✖ Map p54, B1

Creatively using Icelandic ingredients with Mediterranean techniques high up on the top of the Harpa concert hall. You can start with a splashy cocktail before digging into spaghetti with local langoustine, or wood-roasted catfish with Parmesan and chilli. (☎519 9700; www.kolabrautin.is; Austurbakki 2, Harpa; mains Ikr3400-5900; ⏱11.30am-2pm & 5.30-10.30pm Mon-Fri, 5.30-10.30pm Sat & Sun)

Grænn Kostur
VEGETARIAN €

18 ✖ Map p54, B3

Tucked away in a small shopping arcade behind Skólavörðustígur, this friendly little cafe serves great-tasting veggie daily specials and raw desserts. (☎552 2028; www.graennkostur.is; Skólavörðustígur 8b; mains Ikr1200-1900; ⏱11.30am-9pm Mon-Sat, 1-9pm Sun; ✎)

🔍 Local Life
The Cheese Shop

It doesn't get more local than this. Head to gourmet cheese shop and deli **Ostabúðin** (Map p54, B3; Cheese Shop; ☎562 2772; Skólavörðustígur 8; mains Ikr1040-1540; ⏱10am-6pm Mon-Thu, to 6.30pm Fri, 11am-4pm Sat) on Monday to Friday from 11.30am to 1.30pm (only those hours!) and you can sit in the back room for the friendly owner's catch of the day, cooked up in either a large portion or a huge portion, accompanied by homemade bread. You can also pick up other local goods, such as terrines and duck confit, on the way out.

Soup Car
SOUP €

19 Map p54, C4

This friendly food truck at the foot of Hallgrímskirkja keeps it simple: there's delicious spicy lamb stew or 'vegan power soup' with fresh bread. Cheerfully painted tables dot the sidewalk for those who want to stick around while they sup. Hours are weather-dependent. (Frakkastígur; soup Ikr690-1000; ⏱11.15am-7pm Jun-Sep)

Sushisamba
FUSION €€€

20 Map p54, B2

The reported location of TomKat's last dinner as a married couple (you can apparently request to sit at their table if you book ahead), Sushisamba puts an international spin on straight-up sushi, alongside meat and seafood mains. (☎568 6600; www.sushisamba. is; Þingholtsstræti 5; mains Ikr1900-6000, multicourse menus Ikr7000-9000; ⏱5-11pm Sun-Thu, to midnight Fri & Sat)

Drinking

KEX Bar
BAR

21 Map p54, D3

Believe it or not, locals flock to this hostel bar-restaurant (mains Ikr1700 to Ikr2500) in an old cookie factory (*kex* means 'cookie') with broad windows facing the sea, an inner courtyard and loads of happy hipsters. The vibe is 1920s Vegas, with saloon doors, an old-school barber station, scuffed floors and happy chatter. (www.kexhostel.is; Skúlagata 28; ⏱noon-11pm; 📶)

Babalú
CAFE

22 Map p54, B3

This mellow cafe feels like the den of one of your eccentric friends. Books and board games abound, and the baked goods, terraces and comfy couches are the main draw. Paninis are just OK, so fill up instead on homemade chocolate cake and apple crumble. (☎555 8845; Skólavörðustígur 22a; ⏱8am-9pm; 📶)

Local Life

The Cafe Scene

The city's ratio of coffeehouses to citizens is staggering. These low-key hang-outs crank up the intensity after hours, when tea is swapped for tipples. Accidental hipsters sporting well-worn *lopapeysur* (Icelandic woollen sweaters) hang in places like **Tíu Droppar** (Ten Drops; Map p54, C3; ☎551 9380; Laugavegur 27; ⏱9am-1am Mon-Thu, 10am-1am Sat & Sun; 📶). One of those quintessential Reykjavík cafes, it's in a cosy teapot-lined basement, and serves waffles, brunches (Ikr640 to Ikr990) and sandwiches, then in the evenings morphs into a wine bar with occasional live music. It's said that the Sunday-night pianist can play anything by ear.

Beer garden along Laugavegur

Reykjavík Roasters CAFE

23 📍 Map p54, C3

This tiny hipster joint is easily spotted on warm days with its smattering of wooden tables and potato sacks dropped throughout the paved square. Swig a perfect latte with a flaky croissant. (www.reykjavikroasters.is; Kárastígur 1; 🕑8am-6pm Mon-Fri, 9am-7pm Sat & Sun)

Kaffi Mokka CAFE

The decor at Reykjavík's oldest coffee shop, next door to Ófeigur Björnsson (see 44 🔒 Map p54, B2), has changed little since the 1950s, and its original mosaic pillars and copper lights either look retro-cool or dead tatty, depending on your mood. The mixed clientele – from older folks to tourists to trendy artists –

dig the selection of sandwiches, cakes and waffles. (📞552 1174; www.mokka.is; Skólavörðustígur 3a; 🕑9am-6.30pm)

Bravó BAR

24 📍 Map p54, B3

Friendly, knowledgeable bartenders, a laid-back vibe with great people-watching, cool tunes on the sound system and happy hour (5pm to 9pm) draught local beers for Ikr500 – what's not to love? (Laugavegur 22; 🕑6.30pm-1am Mon-Thu, to 4.30am Fri & Sat; 🛜)

C is for Cookie CAFE

25 📍 Map p54, B3

Named in honour of *Sesame Street*'s Cookie Monster, this cheerful spot has super coffee, plus great homemade cakes, salad, soup and grilled sandwiches. (Týsgata 8; ⏱7.30am-6pm Mon-Fri, 11am-5pm Sat, noon-5pm Sun)

Kaffifélagið   CAFE

26 🚇 Map p54, B2

A popular hole-in-the-wall for a quick cuppa on the run, with a couple of outdoor tables, too. (Skólavörðustígur 10; ⏱7.30am-6pm Mon-Fri, 10am-4pm Sat)

Lebowski Bar   BAR

27 🚇 Map p54, B3

Named after the eponymous 'Dude' of moviedom, the grungy Lebowski Bar

Local Life

Casual Grub

Visit the local pub **Vitabar** (Map p54, C4; Bergþórugata 21; mains Ikr900-1600; ⏱11.30am-11pm, bar to 1am or 2am Fri & Sat), on a quiet residential street, for delicious hamburgers and hand-cut fries. Perfect with a pint. **Noodle Station** (Map p54, B3; 📞551 3199; Skólavörðustígur 21a; mains Ikr1190; ⏱11am-10pm Mon-Fri, noon-10pm Sat & Sun) is a perennial favourite for no-frills noodle soups of ambiguously Asian origin.

There's no sign, but those in the know come to **Hverfisgata 12** (Map p54, B2; 📞437 0203; Hverfisgata 12; pizzas Ikr2100-2800; ⏱11.30am-11pm, 👣), in a cream-coloured converted corner house with fabulous family-style ambience, for some of the city's best pizzas.

is smack in the middle of the action with Americana smothering the walls, and loads of White Russians (from Ikr1500) – a favourite from the film. (Laugavegur 20a; ⏱11.30am-1am Sun-Thu, to 4am Fri & Sat)

Bast   BAR

28 🚇 Map p54, B2

A young, happy post-work crowd fills this warehouse-like space hosting good DJs. (📞519 7579; www.bast.is; Hverfisgata 20; ⏱11am-midnight Mon-Wed, to 1am Thu-Sat, to 8pm Sun)

Entertainment

Bíó Paradís   CINEMA

29 ⭐ Map p54, C3

This totally cool cinema, decked out in movie posters and vintage officeware, screens specially curated Icelandic films with English subtitles. It's a chance to see movies that you may not find elsewhere. Plus there's a happy hour from 5pm to 7.30pm. (www.bio-paradis.is; Hverfisgata 54; adult Ikr1600; 📶)

Café Rosenberg   LIVE MUSIC

30 ⭐ Map p54, C2

This big, book-lined storefront, with broad-paned windows looking out onto the street, is dotted with couches and cocktail tables, and hosts all manner of live acts, from local singer-songwriters to jazz groups. (📞551 2442; Klapparstígur 25-27; ⏱3pm-1am Mon-Thu, 4pm-2am Fri & Sat)

National Theatre

THEATRE

31 ⭐ Map p54, B2

The National Theatre has three separate stages and puts on plays, musicals and operas, from modern Icelandic works to Shakespeare. (Þjóðleikhúsið; ☎551 1200; www.leikhusid.is; Hverfisgata 19; ☺closed Jul)

Shopping

Kiosk

CLOTHING

32 🅰 Map p54, D3

This wonderful designers' cooperative is lined with creative women's fashion in a glass-fronted boutique. Designers take turns (wo)manning the store. (☎445 3269; Laugavegur 65; ☺10am-6pm Mon-Fri, 11am-5pm Sat, 1-4pm Sun Jun-Aug, reduced hours Sep-May)

KronKron

CLOTHING, SHOES

33 🅰 Map p54, D3

This is where Reykjavík goes high fashion, with the likes of Marc Jacobs and Vivienne Westwood making an appearance. But we really enjoy the Scandinavian designers (including Kron by KronKron) offering silk dresses, knit capes, scarves and even wool underwear. The handmade shoes are off the charts and are also sold down the street at **Kron,** located at Laugavegur 48. (☎562 8388; www. kronkron.com; Laugavegur 63b; ☺10am-6pm Mon-Fri, to 5pm Sat)

Mál og Menning

BOOKS

34 🅰 Map p54, B3

Friendly, popular and well-stocked independent bookshop carries great English-language books for getting under the skin of Iceland. Check out *Thermal Pools in Iceland* by Jón G Snæland and Þóra Sigurbjörnsdóttir; you can browse it in the lively cafe. Also sells CDs, games and newspapers. (☎580 5000; Laugavegur 18; ☺9am-10pm Mon-Fri, 10am-10pm Sat)

Handknitting Association of Iceland

CLOTHING

35 🅰 Map p54, B3

Traditional handmade hats, socks and sweaters are sold at this knitting collective, or you can buy yarn, needles and knitting patterns and do it yourself. The association has a smaller **branch** at Laugavegur 53b that sells made-up items only. (Handprjónasamband Íslands; ☑552 1890; www.handknit.is; Skólavörðustígur 19; ☺9am-9pm Mon-Fri, to 6pm Sat, 10am-6pm Sun)

Leynibuðin
CLOTHING

36 🔒 Map p54, C3

A consortium of young designers, Leynibuðin is a veritable minimarket of locally crafted apparel. Items border on hipster and grunge – it's a great introduction to the city's made-at-home trend. (www.leynibudin.is; Laugavegur 55; ☺11am-6pm Mon-Fri)

Skúma Skot
ARTS & CRAFTS

37 🔒 Map p54, C3

Nine designers create unique handmade porcelain items, women's and kids' clothing, paintings and cards. It's in a tiny house behind the Booking Lounge travel agency. (☑663 1013; Laugavegur 23; ☺10am-6pm Tue-Fri, to 4pm Sat & Sun)

Spark
ARTS & CRAFTS

38 🔒 Map p54, B3

This gallery and shop has a rotating selection of unique local designers. You can expect art and knitwear, and look out for the fishbone model-making kit! (☑552 2656; www.sparkdesignspace.com; Klapparstígur 33; ☺10am-6pm Mon-Fri, noon-4pm Sat)

Álafoss
CLOTHING

39 🔒 Map p54, B2

Loads of hand- or machine-made *lopapeysur* (Icelandic woollen sweaters) and other wool products. Their **outlet store** in Mosfellsbær also sells yarn and needles. (☑562 6303; www.alafoss.is; Laugavegur 8; ☺9am-10pm)

Geysir
CLOTHING

40 🔒 Map p54, B3

For traditional Icelandic goods, Geysir boasts an elegant selection of sweat-

---

🔍 Local Life

Outdoors Outfitters

Iceland's premier outdoor-clothing company **66° North** (Map p54, B2; ☑535 6680; www.66north.is; Bankastræti 5; ☺9am-10pm) began by making all-weather wear for Arctic fishermen. This metamorphosed into costly, fashionable streetwear: jackets, fleeces, hats and gloves.

If you're looking to outfit for hiking or camping, your best bet is **Gangleri Outfitters** (Map p54, D3; ☑583 2222; www.outfitters.is; Hverfisgata 82; ☺10am-7pm Mon-Fri, 11am-5pm Sat & Sun), with camping gear sales and rentals: tents, sleeping bags, stoves, backpacks, boots, climbing gear, GPS etc.

Fjallakofinn (Map p54, B2; ☑510 9505; www.fjallakofinn.is; Laugavegur 11; ☺9am-7pm Mon-Fri, 10am-4pm Sat, noon-5pm Sun) offers (pricey) brand-name camping and climbing gear, GoPros and more, plus equipment rental.

ers, blankets and men's and women's clothes, shoes and bags. (☎519 6000; www.geysir.com; Skólavörðustígur 16; ⊙10am-10pm)

Aurum JEWELLERY

41 🔒 Map p54, B2

Guðbjörg at Aurum is one of Reykjavík's more interesting designers; her delicate silver jewellery is sophisticated stuff, its shapes often inspired by leaves and flowers. (☎551 2770; Bankastræti 4; ⊙10am-6pm Mon-Fri, 11am-5pm Sat)

Viking SOUVENIRS

42 🔒 Map p54, B2

You can't miss this crammed souvenir shop with giant trolls out front and tourists thronging through the trinket-filled store. It also has a branch at Hafnarstræti 1. (www.theviking.is; Laugavegur 1; ⊙9am-10pm)

Volcano CLOTHING

43 🔒 Map p54, C3

This design shop focuses on women's fashion, playing with textures and creating an interesting layered feel. Everything is locally made and designed with all ages and shapes in mind. (☎588 0100; www.volcanodesign.is; Laugavegur 40; ⊙11am-6pm Mon-Fri, to 5pm Sat)

Ófeigur Björnsson CLOTHING, JEWELLERY

44 🔒 Map p54, B2

Ófeigur Björnsson and other local goldsmiths make jewellery with lava

✓ Top Tip

Shopping Icelandic Style

▶ Reykjavík's vibrant design culture makes for great shopping: from sleek, fish-skin purses and knitted *lopapeysur* (Icelandic woollen sweaters) to unique music or lip-smacking Icelandic schnapps *brennivín*.

▶ Laugavegur is the most dense shopping street. You'll find interesting shops all over town, but fashion concentrates near the Frakkastígur and Vitastígur end of Laugavegur.

▶ Skólavörðustígur is strong for arts and jewellery. Bankastræti and Austurstræti have many touristy shops.

▶ Don't forget – all visitors are eligible for a **15% tax refund** on their shopping, under certain conditions (see p141).

and other natural materials. Hildur Bolladóttir is a master dressmaker and also shows modern bags and felted hats. There's an art gallery upstairs. (☎551 1161; www.ofeigur.is; Skólavörðustígur 5; ⊙10am-6pm Mon-Sat)

Annaranna CLOTHING

45 🔒 Map p54, D3

This new boutique carries high-quality, youthful clothes and accessories in a bright store on Reykjavík's main shopping street. (☎551 6565; www.annaranna.is; Laugavegur 77; ⊙10am-6pm Mon-Fri, to 5pm Sat)

Local Life
Laugardalur

The verdant park at Laugardalur, 4km east of the centre, was once the main source of Reykjavík's hot water: Laugardalur means 'Hot Springs Valley', and you'll still find relics from the old wash house. Laugardalur is a favourite of locals for its huge geothermal swimming complex, spa, arenas, skating rink, botanical gardens, cafe and kids' zoo and entertainment park. Nearby are top museums and a farmers market.

Getting There

🚌 **Bus** 2, 14, 15, 17 and 19 pass 200m from Laugardalur park; 14 is closest to the pool.

🚌 **Bus** 5 serves the waterfront and Sigurjón Ólafsson Museum.

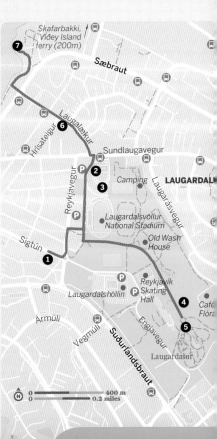

❶ Local Art

Visit Ásmundur Sveinsson's playful sculptures at Reykjavík Art Museum's **Ásmundarsafn** (Ásmundur Sveinsson Museum; ☏553 2155; www.artmuseum.is; Sigtún; adult/child Ikr1300/free; ⏱10am-5pm May-Sep, 1-5pm Oct-Apr). Monumental concrete creations fill the garden, while inside are works in wood, clay and metals. Visit the dome: acoustics create the museum's 'must-sing policy'.

❷ Hot Springs

Reykjavík's naturally hot water is the heart of the city's social life. **Laugardalslaug** (Sundlaugavegur 30a; adult/child Ikr600/130, suit/towel rental Ikr800/550; ⏱6.30am-10pm Mon-Fri, 8am-10pm Sat & Sun; 👶) has the largest, best facilities: Olympic-sized pools, seven hot-pots, saltwater tub, steam bath and curling 86m water slide.

❸ Workout & Pampering

Super-duper **Laugar Spa** (☏553 0000; www.laugarspa.is; Sundlaugavegur 30a; day pass Ikr4990; ⏱6am-10.30pm Mon-Fri, 8am-10pm Sat, to 8pm Sun) offers six saunas and steam rooms; a seawater tub; a vast, well-equipped gym; a cafe; fitness classes; and beauty and massage clinics. The spa is 18+ and includes access to Laugardalslaug.

❹ Gourmet Gardens

The **Reykjavík Botanic Gardens** (Grasagarður; www.grasagardur.is; admission free; ⏱10am-10pm May-Sep, to 5pm Oct-Apr) contain over 5000 varieties of sub-Arctic plant species, colourful seasonal flowers and bird life, and a wonderful summer cafe, **Café Flóra** (Flóran; ☏553 8872; www.floran.is; cakes Ikr850, mains Ikr950-2500; ⏱10am-10pm Jun-Aug; 🖉).

❺ Family Fun

The **Reykjavík Zoo & Family Park** (Fjölskyldu og Húsdýragarðurinn; ☏575 7800; www.mu.is; adult/child Ikr750/550, 1-/10-/20-ride ticket Ikr270/2300/4300; ⏱10am-6pm Jun–mid-Aug, to 5pm mid-Aug–May; 👶) gets packed with happy local families. Don't expect lions; think seals, foxes and farm animals. The family park section has a mini-racetrack, child-size bulldozers, a giant trampoline, boats and rides.

❻ Shop Local

Frú Lauga (☏534 7165; www.frulauga.is; Laugalækur 6; ⏱11am-6pm Mon-Fri, to 4pm Sat; 🖉) farmers market sources its products from all over the countryside. Sample *skyr* desserts from Erpsstaðir farm, organic vegetables, meats, curated international chocolates, wine and the like. There's also a **city centre branch** (Map p54, B3; ☏534 7185; www.frulauga.is; Óðinsgata 1; ⏱11am-6pm Mon-Fri, to 4pm Sat; 🖉).

❼ Waterfront Sculpture & Walks

The peaceful seafront studio of sculptor Sigurjón Ólafsson (1908–82) is now the **Sigurjón Ólafsson Museum** (Listasafn Sigurjóns Ólafssonar; ☏553 2906; www.lso.is; Laugarnestangi 70; adult/child Ikr500/free; ⏱2-5pm Tue-Sun Jun–mid-Sep, 2-5pm Sat & Sun mid-Sep–Nov & Feb-May), showcasing his powerful busts and driftwood totem poles.

Local Life
Viðey Island

Getting There

⛴ **Ferry** It's only five minutes from Skarfabakki to, 4.5km east of the city centre.

🚌 **Bus** 5 stops near Skarfabakki; on the hop-on-hop-off tour bus route.

On fine-weather days, the tiny uninhabited island of Viðey (www.videy.com) makes a wonderful day trip. You can enjoy Tuesday-evening cultural tours with varying themes in summer, while in late August, some Reykjavikers come to pick wild caraway. Less than 1km off Reykjavík's Skarfabakki harbour, it feels a world away. Surprising modern artworks, an abandoned village and great bird-watching add to its remote spell. The only sounds are the wind, the waves and golden bumblebees buzzing among the tufted vetch and hawkweed.

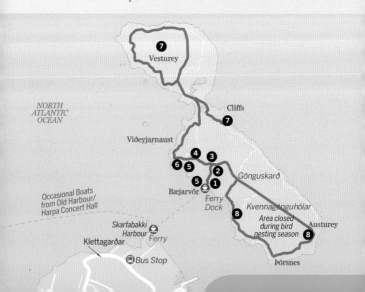

1 Local History

Viðey was settled around AD900 and farmed until the 1950s. It was home to a powerful monastery from 1225, but in 1539 it was wiped out by Danish soldiers during the Reformation. When you arrive, look for a **monument to Skúli Magnússon** (1711–94), the powerful sheriff who built his home here in the 1750s. He's buried here.

2 Viðeyarstofa & Church

Iceland's oldest stone house, **Viðeyarstofa** was the residence of Skúli Magnússon. It now houses a **cafe** (mains Ikr800-2900; 🕙11.30am-6pm Wed-Mon, to 8pm Tue mid-May–Sep, 1.30-4pm Sat & Sun Oct–mid-May) serving goodies like salmon, mussels and waffles. Explore the display of local finds in the basement, the 18th-century wooden **church** and the ancient **monastery foundations**.

3 Explore the Island

The whole island is criss-crossed with walking paths. Some you can bicycle, others are more precarious. A good map at the harbour shows which are which. The island is great for **birdwatching** (30 species breed here) and **botany** (over one-third of all Icelandic plants grow on the island).

4 Bike It!

In summer you can hire a **bike** (2/5hr rental Ikr2500/3500; 🕙Jun-Aug) or bring your own, or come with a **Bike Company** (📞590 8550; www.bikecompany.is; Bankastræti 2; bike rental per 5hr Ikr3500; 🕙9am-5pm Mon-Fri) tour. There's nothing quite like the free, wind-in-your-hair feeling of cycling along the island paths.

5 Wander the Art

Visit Ólafur Eliasson's panelled art installation **The Blind Pavilion** (2003) and Yoko Ono's **Imagine Peace Tower** (2007), a 'wishing well' that blasts a dazzling column of light into the sky every night between 9 October (John Lennon's birthday) and 8 December (the anniversary of his death). See Viðey's website for **Peace Tower tours** from Reykjavík.

6 Barbecue

Locals in the know come prepared with cook-out supplies and head to glass-fronted **Viðeyjarnaust cabin**, on a beautiful headland, which has a public barbecue.

7 To the North

Trails leading northwest take you around ponds, some monuments to shipwrecks, the low **cliffs of Eiðisbjarg**, and **Vesturey** at the northern tip of the island. Richard Serra's huge basalt sculptures, **Áfangar** (Milestones; 1990), dot this part of the island.

8 Southern Ruins

Trails to the southeast lead past the natural sheepfold **Réttin**, the tiny grotto **Paradíshellir** (Paradise Cave), and then to the **abandoned fishing village** at Sundbakki. Most of the south coast is a protected area, closed to visitors from May to June.

Top Experiences
Blue Lagoon

Getting There

🚌 **Bus** Reykjavík Excursions (www.re.is) connects Reykjavík, the airport and the lagoon.

🚌 **Bus** Reykjanes Express (www.reykjanesexpress.is) bus GRI for Reykjavík's BSÍ Terminal & Grindavík

In a magnificent black lava field 47km southwest of Reykjavík (between Keflavík and Grindavík), this milky-teal spa is fed by water (at a perfect 38°C) from futuristic Svartsengi geothermal plant. Those who say it's too expensive, too commercial and too crowded aren't wrong, but you'll be missing something special if you don't go. The colour and feel of the water is truly otherworldly, and with the roiling steam clouds and people daubed in white silica mud, you'll feel you're on another planet.

Don't Miss

A Good Soak

The superheated spawater (70% sea water, 30% fresh water) is rich in blue-green algae, mineral salts and fine silica mud, which condition and exfoliate the skin – sounds like advertising speak, but you really do come out as soft as a baby's bum.

Explore the Complex

The lagoon has an enormous complex of changing rooms, restaurants, a rooftop viewpoint and gift shop. At the pool you'll find hot-pots, steam rooms, sauna, bar and a piping-hot waterfall that delivers a powerful hydraulic massage – like being pummelled by a troll. A VIP section has its own wading space, lounge and viewing platform.

Massage

For extra relaxation, lie on a floating mattress and have a massage therapist knead your knots (half-/one hour €60/95). Book spa treatments well in advance; look online for packages and winter rates.

Stay Longer

If you thrive on remote lava fields and extensive spa time, **Blue Lagoon – Clinic Hotel** (☏420 8806; www.bluelagoon.com; s/d incl breakfast Ikr38,500/46,200; @🖰) and **Northern Light Inn** (☏426 8650; www.northernlightinn.is; s/d incl breakfast Ikr26,500/34,500; @🖰) are both walking distance from the lagoon.

Nearby: Cycle & Quad

Combine your Blue Lagoon visit with myriad package tours; or, hook up with nearby **ATV Adventures** (☏857 3001; www.atv4x4.is) for ATV (from Ikr9900 per seat) or cycling tours (Ikr9900 from the lagoon through the lava fields), or bicycle rental (per four/eight hours Ikr2900/3900). They pickup and dropoff at the lagoon.

Bláa Lónið

☏420 8800

www.bluelagoon.com

Jun-Aug admission adult/14 -15 yr/under 14 yr from €40/20/free, visitor pass €10

🕑9am-9pm Jun & 11-31 Aug, to 11pm Jul-10 Aug, 10am-8pm Sep-May

---

☑ Top Tips

▶ Cut long lines and get e-ticket deals (www.bluelagoon.com) or tour company vouchers (Iceland Air, Reykjavík Excursions).

▶ Avoid summertime between 10am to 2pm – go early or after 7pm.

▶ Carpark has luggage check (Ikr300/day/bag).

✕ Take a Break

On-site **Blue Café** (snacks Ikr780-1950; 🕑9am-10pm Jun-Aug, to 9pm Sep-May) has cafeteria-style eats, while **LAVA Restaurant** (lunch/dinner mains Ikr3950/5900; 🕑noon-10pm Jul-mid Aug, to 8.30pm or 9pm rest of year) features Icelandic dishes.

Local Life
Reykjanes Peninsula

Getting There

🚗 **Car** Best way to travel.

🚌 **Bus** Reykjanes Express bus 4 serves Garður and Sandgerði; bus GRI connects Reykjavík's BSÍ terminal, the Blue Lagoon and Grindavík.

The Reykjanes Peninsula (www.visitreykjanes.is) is special not only for the Blue Lagoon, Iceland's most famous attraction, but for other local favourites. Sweet fishing hamlets Garður and Sandgerði sit minutes to the west of the airport. Untamed landscapes of volcanic craters, mineral lakes, hot springs and rugged, ATV-ready mountains and coastal lava fields stretch from Reykjanestá to the Reykjanesfólkvangur Wilderness Reserve.

❶ Garður

Garður's beautiful windswept **Garðsk-agi headland** is great for **birdwatching** and sometimes seal or **whale spotting**. Two quaint **lighthouses** add drama. Balconied **2 Lighthouses Restaurant** (Tveir Vitar; ☎422 7214; Garðurbraut 100; mains Ikr1950-5000; ⏱8am-noon Mon, to 10pm Tue-Thu, to 11pm Fri, 10am-11pm Sat, 10am-10pm Sun Apr-Oct) has superb views to Snæfellsjökull.

❷ Local History & Seafood

In Sandgerði, peruse the fascinating exhibit about shipwrecked explorer Jean-Baptiste Charcot at the **Sudurnes Science and Learning Center** (☎423 7551; http://thekkingarsetur.is/english/exhibitions/; Gerðavegur 1; adult/child Ikr600/300; ⏱10am-4pm Mon-Fri, 1-5pm Sat & Sun May-Sep, 10am-2pm Mon-Fri Oct-Apr). Enjoy a seafood lunch at excellent **Vitinn** (☎423 7755; www.vitinn.is; Vitatorg 7; mains Ikr4100-6850; ⏱11.30am-9pm May-Sep, reduced hours Oct-Apr).

❸ Birds & Bards

Pleasant **beaches** dot the coast south of Sandgerði, and the surrounding marshes are frequented by more than 190 species of **birds**. You'll find a lonely church at **Hvalsnes**, featured in a famous Icelandic hymn by Hall-grímur Pétursson (1616–74), written at the death of his young daughter who was buried here.

❹ 100 Crater Park

In the far southwest of the peninsula, the lava fields and wild volcanic craters are dubbed 100 Crater Park.

Power plants exploit geothermal heat to produce salt from seawater and to generate electricity. **Power Plant Earth** (Orkuverið Jörð; ☎436 1000; www.powerplantearth.is; admission Ikr1000; ⏱12.30-4.30pm Sat & Sun Jun-Sep) has an interactive exhibition about energy.

❺ Valahnúkur

One of the most wild and wonderful spots on the peninsula is the lava fields at Valahnúkur. Dramatic, climbable **cliffs** and **Reykjanesviti lighthouse** sit near a multicoloured geothermal area with hot spring **Gunnuhver**.

❻ Break in Grindavík

For a late-afternoon pick-me-up, stop off at charming dock-front cafe **Bryggjan** (snacks Ikr600-1400; ⏱8am-11pm Mon-Fri, 10am-11pm Sat & Sun; 🛜), in Grindavík.

❼ Open Air

To explore Reykjanes by foot, ATV or horse, Grindavík is home to outfitters **ATV Adventures** (☎857 3001; www.atv4x4.is) and **Arctic Horses** (☎848 0143; www.arctichorses.is; Hópsheiði 16, Grindavík), and the **tourist office** (☎420 1190; www.visitgrindavik.is; ⏱10am-5pm mid-May–mid-Sep) stocks maps of the region's walking trails.

❽ Springs, Lava & Lakes

Looping back to Reykjavík, visit either the **Blue Lagoon** (p70), late, like the locals, or the dramatic lava, hot springs and lakes around the 300-sq-km **Rey-kjanesfólkvangur Wilderness Reserve**.

Explore

Golden Circle

The Golden Circle takes in three marquee attractions all within 100km of the capital: Þingvellir, Geysir and Gullfoss. It's an artificial tourist circuit (no natural topography marks its extent), loved by thousands. You'll see a meeting point of the continental plates and site of the ancient parliament (Þingvellir), a spouting hot spring (Geysir) and a roaring waterfall (Gullfoss), all in one doable-in-a-day loop.

The Region in a Day

☀ Get an early start from Reykjavík and head straight to **Þingvellir** (p76), planning at least an hour to wander the parliament site, the rift and falls. On your way there you can visit the **Gljúfrasteinn Laxness Museum** (p84), the home of Nobel Prize-winning author Halldór Laxness.

☀ Lunch on delicious wild-caught dishes in Laugarvatn at **Lindin** (p86), in its formal restaurant or laid-back bistro. Or head to **Efstidalur II** (p86) for local-caught fish and farm burgers; don't miss the farm ice cream and cool barn cafe. It also has horse riding. For a swank spa experience, take a dip at **Fontana** (p83). Then visit **Geysir** (p78) and **Gullfoss** (p80). If time permits, squeeze in **river rafting** (p86) near Reykholt.

☾ If you didn't hit the spa at Fontana be sure to spend your evening in Flúðir at **Gamla Laugin** (p83), a natural historic geothermal pool, newly and wonderfully refurbished, next to mini-geysers, meadows and a rushing brook. Afterwards, grab a bite at **Minilik Ethiopian Restaurant** (p86), or stop in Selfoss at **Tryggvaskála** (p87) for more formal Icelandic fare.

◉ Top Experiences

Þingvellir (p76)

Geysir (p78)

Gullfoss (p80)

♥ Best of Golden Circle

Eating
Lindin (p86)

Silfra Restaurant (p77)

For Free
Þingvellir (p76)

Geysir (p78)

Gullfoss (p80)

Getting There

🚗 **Car** Easiest way to tailor your trip.

⊙ **Tour** Myriad tours cover the Golden Circle.

🚌 **Bus** Key routes: **Reykjavík Excursions** (☎580 5400; www.re.is) bus 6/6A (BSÍ terminal–Þingvellir–Laugarvatn–Geysir–Gullfoss, one daily mid-June to mid-September) and **Sterna** (☎551 1166; www.sterna.is) bus F35/F35A (Harpa–Þingvellir–Laugarvatn–Geysir–Gullfoss–Kjölur Highlands–Kerlingarfjöll–Akureyri, one daily late June to early September).

Top Experiences
Þingvellir

UNESCO World Heritage Site Þingvellir National Park (23km east of Reykjavík) is Iceland's most important historical spot and a place of vivid beauty. The Viking settlers established the world's first democratic parliament, the Alþingi, here in AD 930. Meetings were conducted outdoors in the superb natural setting: an immense, fissured rift valley caused by the meeting of the North American and Eurasian tectonic plates, with rivers and waterfalls all around.

👁 Map p82, B2

www.thingvellir.is

Öxarárfoss falls

Don't Miss

Tectonic Plates

Þingvellir sits on a tectonic plate boundary where North America and Europe are tearing away from each other at 1mm to 18mm per year. As a result, the plain is scarred by dramatic fissures, ponds and rivers, including the great rift **Almannagjá**. A path runs along the fault between the clifftop visitors centre and the Alþingi site. Look for the **Öxarár-foss** falls, on the northern edge of the cliffs.

Historic Buildings

The farmhouse in the bottom of the rift, **Þing-vallabær**, was built for the 1000th anniversary of the Alþingi in 1930 by state architect Guðjón Samúelsson. It's now used as the park warden's office and prime minister's summer house. **Þing-vallakirkja** was one of Iceland's first churches. The original was consecrated in the 11th century; the current building dates from 1859.

Encampment Ruins

Straddling the Öxará river are ruins of temporary camps called *búðir* (booths). These stone founda-tions were covered during sessions and also acted like stalls at today's music festivals: selling beer, food and vellum. Most date to the 17th and 18th centuries; the largest, and one of the oldest, is **Biskupabúð**, north of the church.

Alþingi

Near the dramatic Almannagjá fault and fronted by a boardwalk is the **Lögberg** (Law Rock), where the Alþingi convened annually, and where the *lögsögumaður* (law speaker) recited existing laws. After Iceland's conversion to Christianity the site shifted to the foot of the Almannagjá cliffs, which acted as a natural amplifier. That site is marked by the Icelandic flag.

☑ Top Tips

▶ Free one-hour guided tours (10am June to August) set off from the church.

▶ **Þingvellir Informa-tion Centre** (Leirar Þjónustumiðstöð; ☏482 2660; www.thingvellir.is; ◷9am-5pm May-Sep), on Rte 36 on the north side of the lake, has details about the park, as does **Þingvellir Visitors Cen-tre** (Gestastofa; ◷9am-5pm) in the south.

▶ Þingvellir is pro-nounced *thing*-vet-lir.

✕ Take a Break

There's not much to eat in the park. There's a basic **cafeteria** (soup Ikr950; ◷9am-10pm Apr-Oct) in the information centre, or the fab new **Silfra Restaurant** (www.ioniceland.is; Nesjavellir vid, Þingvallavatn; dinner mains Ikr4400-6200; ◷11.30am-10pm) at the Ion Luxury Adventure Hotel (on the south side of Þingvallavatn) features slow-food ingredients and a bar with plate-glass windows.

Top Experiences
Geysir

One of Iceland's most famous tourist attractions, Geysir (pronounced *gay*-zeer, which literally means 'gusher') is the original hot-water spout after which all other geysers are named. Discovered in the beautiful Haukadalur geothermal region, which is surrounded by verdant fields, the Great Geysir has been active for perhaps 800 years, and once gushed water up to 80m into the air. Now relatively dormant, its neighbour Strokkur steals the show with steady eruptions that make crowds oooh and aaah.

Map p82, D1

admission free

Strokkur

Don't Miss

Geysir & Strokkur

Geysir has gone through periods of lessened activity since around 1916. Earthquakes can stimulate activity, though nowadays eruptions are rare. Luckily for visitors, the reliable geyser, **Strokkur**, sits alongside. You'll rarely wait more than 10 minutes for it to shoot an impressive 15m to 30m plume before vanishing down its enormous hole.

Geysir Center

The large **Geysir Center** (☑ 480 6800; www.geysircenter.com; ☉ 10am-10pm Jun-Aug, to 6pm Sep-May) corrales the masses across the street from the geysers. A souvenir shop of mall-like proportions with Icelandic name brands, and an N1 petrol station, share space with eateries and **Geysirstofa** (☑ 480 6800; admission free; ☉ 10am-5pm May-Aug, noon-4pm Sep-Apr), an interesting audiovisual exhibition about geysers, volcanoes and earthquakes.

Surrounding Activities

Enjoy Geysir's picturesque setting by hiking in nearby Haukadalur forest, hitting the links at **Geysir Golf Course** (Haukadalsvöllur; ☑ 893 8733; www.geysirgolf.is; 9 holes Ikr3000) or going salmon fishing on the Tungufljót river. On cold, clear winter evenings, look out for the Northern Lights. Many tours from Reykjavík offer these activities and more.

Adventure Tours

Iceland Safari (☑ 544 5454; www.icelandsafari.com), 1km south of Geysir, takes super-Jeep trips to places throughout the southwest. Or go 4km east of Geysir to Kjóastaðir horse farm where **Geysir Hestar** (☑ 847 1046; www.geysirhestar.com; Kjóastaðir 2) offers horse riding in the area or along Hvítará Canyon to Gullfoss. **Rafting trips** (p86) ply the nearby Hvítá river.

☑ Top Tips

▶ Stand downwind only if you want a shower.

▶ The undulating, hissing geothermal area containing Strokkur and Geysir was free to enter at the time of research, though there is discussion of instituting a fee.

▶ You can grab arresting photos from up the valley, looking back at the volcanic hills and erupting geyser.

✗ Take a Break

The **Geysir Center** houses a massive restaurant (mains Ikr1490 to Ikr2450), cafe (mains Ikr1480 to Ikr2000) and fast-food joint (Ikr990 to Ikr1690).

Across the street, the restaurant at **Hótel Geysir** (☑ 480 6800; www.geysircenter.is; s/d from Ikr22,000/25,000, campsites per person Ikr1500, buffet lunch Ikr3500, dinner mains Ikr2700-5700; ☉ Feb-Dec, campsite May-Sep; @ ☎) bustles with tour groups tucking into the buffet lunch.

Top Experiences
Gullfoss

Iceland's most famous waterfall, Gullfoss (Golden Falls) is a spectacular double cascade dropping a dramatic 32m. As it descends, it kicks up tiered walls of spray before thundering away down a narrow rocky ravine. On sunny days the mist creates shimmering rainbows, and it's also magical in winter when the falls glitter with ice. Though it's a popular sight, the falls' remote location still makes you feel the ineffable forces of nature that have been at work on this landscape for millennia.

⊙ Map p82, D1

www.gullfoss.is

admission free

Don't Miss

Views & Photo Ops

A tarmac path leads from the main parking lot and visitor centre to a grand **lookout** over the falls. Stairs then continue down to the level of the falls. Or, drive in on the spur below the tourist centre at falls level to disabled-accessible parking (only). A path then continues down the valley toward the thundering falls for the most kinetic video shots.

Saving the Falls

Sigríður Tómassdóttir (1871–1957) and her sisters made the first stairs to the falls, guiding people through formerly impassable terrain. In 1907, foreign investors wanted to dam the Hvítá river, which feeds the falls, for a hydroelectric project. Sigríður's father, Tómas Tómasson, only leased them the land, but the developers got permission from the government. Sigríður walked (barefoot!) to Reykjavík to protest. When the investors failed to pay the lease, the agreement was nullified and the falls escaped destruction. Gullfoss was donated to the nation, and since 1979 it's been a nature reserve. Look for the **memorial** to Sigríður near the foot of the stairs from the visitors centre.

Nearby: The Kjölur Route

Gullfoss is the final stop on traditional Golden Circle tours. You can continue along magnificent Rte F35 beyond the falls (the Kjölur Route) for 14.8km while it's paved, after which you need to have a 4WD. Or, take a Reykjavík–Akureyri bus, which stops at the Kerlingarfjöll hiking area as well, such as **Reykjavík Excursions** (📞580 5400; www.re.is) bus 610 or 610A, or **Sterna** (📞551 1166; www.sterna.is) bus F35 or F35A.

☑ Top Tips

▶ On grey, drizzly days, mist can envelop the second drop, making Gullfoss slightly less thrilling.

▶ There's accommodation a few kilometres before the falls at **Hótel Gullfoss** (📞486 8979; www.hotelgullfoss.is; d incl breakfast Ikr24,700; 📶), where clean en suite rooms overlook the moors (get one facing the valley), and there are two hot pots and a restaurant (mains Ikr2100 to Ikr5000) with sweeping views.

✗ Take a Break

Above Gullfoss and next to the main parking lot, a small **tourist information centre, shop and cafe** (www.gullfoss.is; cafe mains Ikr750-1890; ⏱9am-9.30pm Jun-Aug, 9am-6pm Sep-May; 📶) is famous for its organic lamb soup, which is made from locally sourced ingredients and comes with refills. It also offers other soups, salads, sandwiches, cakes and coffee.

Sprengisandur

Kerlingarfjöll (45km) →

Gullfoss

Gjáin
Hrauneyjar (15km)
Burfell
Stöng
Burfell (669m)
Hydroelectric Power Station
Hjálparfoss
26

Leirubakki
268

F338
F35
Bratthólt
Haukadalur
Geysir
Brúarhlöð
Drumboddsstaðir
30
35
Reykholt
Fludir
⊙ 1
Gamla
Laugin
Árnes
32
Vatnsá
272
Hekluhestar
271
Árbakki
Skjaldbreiður (1060m)
Bjarnarfell (72m)
37
Efstadalsfjall (627m)
✕ 6
358
355
✕ 8
Laugarás
Skálholt
Laugin
31
Sólheimar
30
Brjánsstaðir
1
Herríðarhóll
26
Hestheimar
Laugaland
Súluholt
Vatnsholt

Whaling Station
Glymur
Botnsdalur
47

N
20 km
10 km
20 miles
10 miles

Information Centre
Hrafnabjörg (763m)
Kálfstindar
Fontana
2 ⊙
Laugarvatn
Langjarvatn
Apavatn
37
Seydisholar
Kerið
5
35

Selfoss
✕ 7
34

Þingvellir
Alþingi
Visitors
Centre
Skálabrekka
361
365
36
Þingvallavatn
GOLDEN CIRCLE
Úlfljótsvatn
Efri-Brú
Ingólfsfjall (551m)
Flói Nature Reserve
Ölfusá
Eyrarbakki
34

Skálafell (3km)
Laxness Horse Riding (10km)
Gljúfrasteinn Laxness Museum (Mosfellsbær; 14km)
360
360
Nesjavellir
435
36
48
Hengill (768m)
1
Reykjadalur
⊙ 4
⊙ 3
Hveragerði
38
Hveravaðið
Núpur
Raufarhólshellir
Bíldsfell

A B C D E
1 2 3 4

Experiences

Gamla Laugin   GEOTHERMAL POOL

1 ◎ Map p82, D3

Get here before the real crowds come! Opened in Flúðir in 2014, this lovely hot spring is a refurbished version of the one the town used informally for years. It's a broad, calm geothermal pool, mist rising, surrounded by natural rocks and with a gravelly bottom. The walking trail along its edge passes the local river and a series of sizzling vents and geysers. Meadows around fill with wildflowers in summer. During off-hours you might have it totally to yourself.

Find it signposted (there's also a sign for Hvammur) down a rutted track on the northern bank of the river Litla-Laxá in Flúðir. (Secret Lagoon; ☎ 555 3351; www.secretlagoon.is; Flúðir; adult/child Ikr2500/free; ⊙1-10pm)

Fontana   GEOTHERMAL POOL

2 ◎ Map p82, C2

This swanky lakeside soaking spot in Laugarvatn boasts three mod wading pools and a cedar-lined steam room that's fed by a naturally occurring vent below. The cool cafe (snacks Ikr500 to Ikr1200) has lake views. You can rent towels or swimsuits (Ikr800) if you left yours at home. (☎486 1400; www.fontana.is; Laugarvatn; adult/child/under 12 yr Ikr3200/1600/free; ⊙10am-11pm Jun-Sep, 1-9pm Mon-Fri, 11am-9pm Sat & Sun Oct-May)

Hverasvæðið   GEOTHERMAL PARK

3 ◎ Map p82, A3

The geothermal park Hverasvæðið, in the centre of Hveragerði, has mudpots and steaming pools where visitors can dip their feet (but no more). You can book ahead for a guided walk to learn about the area's unique geology and greenhouse power. Or they'll give you an egg and apparatus (Ikr100) for boiling it in the steaming vents. There's a small cafe with geothermally baked bread. (☎483 4601; Hveramörk 13, Hveragerði; adult/child Ikr200/free; ⊙9am-6pm Mon-Sat, 10am-4pm Sun)

Reykjadalur   GEOTHERMAL SITE

4 ◎ Map p82, A3

Reykjadalur is a delightful geothermal valley where there's a bathable hot river – bring your swimsuit. There are maps at the tourist office to find the trail; from the trailhead car park, it's a 3km hike through fields of sulphur-belching plains. Stick to marked paths, lest you melt your shoes, and leave no trash. In recent years the area

---

☑ Top Tip

Circle vs Ring

Don't confuse the Golden Circle with the Ring Road (Rte 1), which wraps around the entire country (and takes a week or more to properly complete).

has taken a beating due to thoughtless visitors. (Hot River Valley)

Kerið
VOLCANO

5 ⊙ Map p82, B3

Around 15.5km north of Selfoss on Rte 35, Kerið is a 6500-year-old explosion crater with vivid red and sienna earth and containing an ethereal green lake. Björk once performed a concert from a floating raft in the middle. At the time of research, local property owners had (controversially) started charging for entrance to Kerið; this may change. (adult/child Ikr350/free; ⊙9am-9pm Jun-Aug)

Gljúfrasteinn Laxness Museum
MUSEUM

Nobel Prize–winning author Halldór Laxness (1902–98) lived in Mosfellsbær all his life. His riverside home is now the Gljúfrasteinn Laxness Museum (off Map p82), easy to visit on the road from Reykjavík to Þingvellir (Rte 36). The author built this upper-class 1950s house and it remains intact with original furniture, writing room and Laxness' fine-art collection (needlework, sweetly, by his wife Auður). An audio-tour leads you round. Look for his beloved Jaguar parked out front. (☎586 8066; www.gljufrasteinn.is; Mosfellsbær; adult/child Ikr800/free; ⊙9am-5pm Jun-Aug, 10am-5pm Tue-Sun Sep-May, closed Sat & Sun Jan-Feb & Nov)

Laxnes
HORSE RIDING

Small, family-owned Laxnes is run by an older couple whose nephews take newbies out for relaxed trots. On the road between Þingvellir and Reykjavík (off Map p82). Also offers combo tours. (☎566 6179; www.laxnes.is; Mosfellsbær)

Laugarvatn Adventures
ROCK CLIMBING, CAVING

Runs two- to three-hour caving and rock-climbing trips in the hills around Laugarvatn (see 2 ⊙ Map p82, C2). (☎862 5614; www.caving.is; Laugarvatn)

☑ Top Tip
Planning Your Journey

▶ Seeing the Golden Circle with your own vehicle allows you to visit at off-hours and explore attractions further afield.

▶ Visiting with a tour, on the other hand, takes out the guesswork. Almost every tour company in Reykjavík offers a Golden Circle excursion.

▶ If you want to spend the night in the relatively small region, Laugarvatn has good services: camp at Þingvellir; luxe it at **Ion Luxury Adventure Hotel** (Map p82, B3; ☎482 3415; www.ioniceland.is; Nesjavellir vid Þingvallavatn; s/d Ikr44,000/51,000; P@🛜♨); or choose from accommodation along Rte 35.

▶ To go on to west Iceland afterwards, complete the Circle backwards, finishing with Þingvellir.

Understand

Supernatural Iceland

Once you see the vast lava fields, eerie natural formations and isolated farms that characterise much of the Icelandic landscape, it should come as no surprise that many Icelanders' beliefs go beyond the scientific.

Hidden People

In the lava are *jarðvergar* (gnomes), *álfar* (elves), *ljósálfar* (fairies), *dvergar* (dwarves), *ljúflingar* (lovelings), *tívar* (mountain spirits) and *englar* (angels). Stories about them have been handed down through generations, and many modern Icelanders claim to have seen these *huldufólk* (hidden people)...or at least to know someone who has.

As in Ireland, there are stories about projects going wrong when workers try to build roads through *huldufólk* homes: the weather turns bad, machinery breaks down, labourers fall ill. In mid-2014 Iceland's 'whimsy factor' again made international news when a road project to link the Álftanes peninsula to the Reykjavík suburb of Garðabær was halted when campaigners warned it would disturb elf habitat.

Ghosts & Trolls

As for Icelandic ghosts, they're substantial beings – not the wafting shadows found elsewhere in Europe. Írafell-Móri (*móri* and *skotta* are used for male and female ghosts, respectively) needed to eat supper every night, and one of the country's most famous spooks, Sel-Móri, got seasick when he stowed away in a boat. Rock stacks and certain lava formations are often said to be trolls, caught out at sunrise and turned forever to stone.

Finding Out More

Surveys suggest that more than half of Icelanders at least entertain the possibility of the existence of *huldufólk*. But a word of warning: many Icelanders get sick of visitors asking, and they don't enjoy the 'Those cute Icelanders! They believe in pixies!' attitude. Even if they don't entirely disbelieve, they're unlikely to admit it to a stranger.

To ask all the questions you want, join a tour in **Hafnarfjörður**, 10km south of Reykjavík, or take a course at the **Icelandic Elf School** (Álfaskólinn; www.elfmuseum.com) in Reykjavík. Yes, there really is such a place, and it runs four-hour introductory classes most Fridays.

Eating

Lindin
ICELANDIC €€

Owned by Baldur, an affable, celebrated chef, Lindin (see 2 ◎ Map p82, C2) is the best restaurant for miles around Laugarvatn. In a sweet little silver house, the restaurant faces the lake and is purely gourmet, with high-concept Icelandic fare featuring local or wild-caught ingredients. The casual, modern bistro serves a more informal menu from soups to an amazing reindeer burger. Book ahead for dinner in high season. (📞486 1262; www.laugarvatn.is; Lindarbraut 2; restaurant mains Ikr3600-5500, bistro mains Ikr1800-4000; ⏰noon-10pm May-Sep, reduced hours Oct-Apr)

Efstidalur II
ICELANDIC €€

6 🍴 Map p82, C2

Located 12km northeast of Laugarvatn on a working dairy farm with brilliant views of hulking Hekla, Efstidalur offers tasty meals and amazing ice cream. The restaurant serves beef from the farm and trout from the lake. The fun ice-cream bar scoops farm ice cream, and has windows looking into the dairy barn. (📞486 1186; www.efstidalur.is; Efstidalur 2; mains Ikr1200-5000; ⏰8am-9pm Jun-Sep)

Minilik Ethiopian Restaurant
ETHIOPIAN €€

Sweet-faced Azeb cooks up traditional Ethiopian specialities in this welcoming, unpretentious spot in Flùðir (see 1 ◎ Map p82, D3). There are loads of vegetarian options, but also lamb such as *awaze tibs* or chicken (*doro kitfo*). As far as we know, this is the only Ethiopian restaurant in Iceland, and it should beckon all lovers of spice. (📞846 9798; www.minilik.is; Flùðir; mains Ikr1850-3000; ⏰noon-8pm Jun-6 Sep; 🍴)

Tryggvaskála
ICELANDIC €€

7 ❌ Map p82, B4

Tryggvaskála's actually worth stopping for. This new restaurant (the brainchild of the Kaffi Krús guys) fills Selfoss' first house (built for bridge workers in 1890). Lovingly renovated and on the riverfront with a romantic mood, the intimate dining rooms are filled with antique touches, and the fine-dining Icelandic menu sources local produce. (☑ 482 1390; www.tryggvaskala.is; Austurvegur 1, Selfoss; mains Ikr2460-5000; ⊙11.30am-10pm)

Varma
ICELANDIC €€

At the Frost & Fire hotel in Hveragerði (see 3 ◉ Map p82, A3) this wonderfully scenic restaurant boasts floor-to-ceiling windows over the stream and gorge. Dishes are Icelandic, using fresh, local ingredients and herbs and often geothermal cooking techniques. (Hveragerði; mains lunch Ikr1670-3700, dinner Ikr3750-5000; ⊙8am-10pm)

Café Mika
INTERNATIONAL €€

8 ❌ Map p82, D2

In Reykholt, Café Mika has an outdoor pizza oven, sandwiches and Icelandic mains, and sells handcrafted chocolate. (☑ 896 6450; Skólabraut 4, Reykholt; mains Ikr1000-3900; ⊙10am-9pm; 🛜)

Grund
ICELANDIC €€

Run by kindly Dagný, this popular restaurant in Flúðir (see 1 ◉ Map p82, D2)

prides itself in offering fresh local food. (☑ 565 9196; www.gistingfludir.is; mains Ikr1750-4900; ⊙11.30am-9pm Jun-mid-Aug)

Shopping

Gallerí Laugarvatn
ARTS & CRAFTS

Local handicrafts, from ironwork to ceramics and woollens, are on offer at this gallery in Laugarvatn (see 2 ◉ Map p82, C2). Also operates a small B&B. (☑ 847 0805; www.gallerilaugarvatn.is; Háholt 1, Laugarvatn; ⊙1-6pm)

☑ Top Tip

Completing the Loop

If you're completing the Golden Circle in the traditional direction starting at Þingvellir, then the route from Gullfoss back to the Ring Road at **Selfoss** and the geothermal fields at **Hveragerði** will be the final stage of your trip. Along the way you'll find plenty to lure you to stop. Most people follow surfaced Rte 35, which passes through **Reykholt** with its river rafting. You can also detour slightly to **Fluðir**, with its geothermal greenhouses and hot spring, and **Skálholt**, once Iceland's religious powerhouse.

If you'd like to continue east rather than return to Reykjavík, see the South Coast chapter (p88).

Explore

South Coast

The Ring Road (Rte 1) sweeps southeast of Reykjavík through wide coastal plains and verdant horse farms before the landscape grows wonderfully jagged, after Hvolsvöllur and Hella, near Skógar and Vík. Inland, mountains thrust upwards, some of them volcanoes wreathed by mist (such as Eyjafjallajökull, site of the 2010 eruption), and awesome glaciers glimmer, as rivers carve their way to black-sand beaches.

The Region in a Day

The south coast is enormous, so you'll need to pick your focus. Head east along the Ring Road, stopping near Hella or Hvolsvöllur for **horse riding** (p93), and Saga studies at **Sögusetrið** (p92); or hit the coast at **Stokkseyri** and **Eyrarbakki** (p92) for a taste of local life in an Icelandic fishing village. If you'd rather explore the powerful Þjórsádalur river valley, go to **Þjórsárstofa** (p96) in Árnes for top sight information. Or, plan a day trip to the **Vestmannaeyjar** (p98) islands.

Lunch at **Gamla Fjósið** (p97) and stop off at **Eyjafjallajökull Visitor Centre** (p96); or head straight along to Skógar, stopping at the several grand **waterfalls** (p95), the **Skógar Folk Museum** (p93) and **Sólheimajökull** (p95) ice tongue. Take any number of **adventure tours** (p95), or zip along to Vík's magnificent coastline at **Dyrhólaey** (p92) and **Reynisfjara** (p92).

In summer book ahead for dinner at Vík's **Suður-Vík** (p98) or **Halldórskaffi** (p98). Definitely reserve ahead to spend the night and see more of this popular part of the country, or power back to Reykjavík.

♥ Best of the South Coast

Natural Wonders

Hekla (p94)

Vatnajökull (p96)

Seljalandsfoss (p95)

Sólheimajökull (p95)

Eyjafjallajökull (p96)

Skógafoss (p95)

Eldfell (p94)

Svartifoss (p96)

Eating

Slippurinn (p98)

Gamla Fjósið (p97)

Getting There

🚗 **Car** Gives the most freedom; roads are good except deep inland.

⊙ **Tours** Almost all Reykjavík-based tour companies offer excursions to the south, and many local operators can also pick up in Reykjavík.

🚌 **Bus** The most popular tourist routes in the country head through here. All companies – **Strætó** (☎540 2700; www.bus.is), **Sterna** (☎551 1166; www.sterna.is) and **Reykjavík Excursions** (☎580 5400; www.re.is) – offer myriad lines. **Trex** (☎587 6000; www.trex.is) serves Þórsmörk and Landmannalaugar.

A → Kerlingarfjöll (45km)

Bjarnarfell (727m)

Gullfoss

Geysir

35 Brúarhlöð

358 30

Flúðir

30

Árnes 8

Þjórsárstofa

26 Leirubakki

Árbakki

272

268

271

12 264

Hella

264

Eyrabakki (45km) 3

Hvolsvöllur

261 Hlíðarendi

255

Seljalandsfoss & Gljúfurárbúi

Bergþórshvoll

253

Atlantsflug

10

Landeyjahöfn

Heimaey

Vestmannaeyjar

Háifoss

Sultartangalón

Bláskógar Hydroelectric Plant

Þjóðveldisbærinn 32 26

Hjálparfoss

Þjórsá

Búrfell (669m)

F225

Þjórsárdalur

Hekla (1491m)

Laufafell

Vatnafjöll

Álftavatn

F210

Tindfjallajökull

Fljótsdalur

Tindfjöll (1251m)

F261

Þórsmörk

Stóra-Mörk III

1

Gljúfurárbúi

5

Seljalandsfoss

Eyjafjallajökull

Valahnúkur (282m)

Fimmvörðuháls

Bakki 247

Ásólfsskáli

Eyjafjallajökull Visitor Centre

Skógafoss

9 **Skógar**

7 4

Skógar Folk Museum 219

Sólheimajökull 6

221

Brekkur

1 2

Dyrhólaey

Reynisfjara

11

Vík

F26

Þórisvatn

Litlisjór

Veiðivötn

F208

Fjallabak Nature Reserve

4WD only

Landmannalaugar Jökuldalur

F208

Kirkjufell

Torfajökull

F208 Lakagí

Eldgjá Gjátin

F210

Mýrdalsjökull

Katla (1250m)

Hafursey (582m)

Mælifell (642m)

Hjörleifshöfði (221m)

Mýrdalssan...

0   20 km
0   10 miles

Vatnajökull

Grænalón

Vatnajökull National Park

E

ngisjór

▲ Fögrufjöll (1090m)

Laki (818m)

Núpsstaðarskógur

Eystrafjall Núpsá

Lómagnúpur (767m) ▲

Skeiðarárjökull

Hvannadalshnúkur (2110m)

Skaftafell

Freysnes ▲

Svínafell

il

Laki Route

Núpsstaður

Sandfell

Öræfajökull

Hof

Öræfi

ℝ Fagrifoss   Foss á Síðu

ℝ

Jökulsárlón (40km)

Hofsnes

F206

Dverghamrar

Kirkjubæjarklaustur

Fjarðrárgljúfur

Skeiðarársandur

Ingólfshöfði

1

Eldhraun

204

NORTH ATLANTIC OCEAN

Kúðafljót

Meðallandssandur

aver

kkvabæjarklaustur

Experiences

Dyrhólaey LANDMARK, WILDLIFE RESERVE

1 ◉ Map p90, C5

One of the south coast's most recognisable natural formations is the rocky plateau and huge stone sea arch at Dyrhólaey (deer-lay), which rises dramatically from the surrounding plain 10km west of Vík, at the end of Rte 218. The promontory is a nature reserve that's rich in bird life, including puffins. It's closed during nesting season (15 May to 25 June), but at other times you can visit its crashing black beaches and get awesome views from atop the archway.

Reynisfjara LANDMARK, BEACH

2 ◉ Map p90, C5

On the west side of **Reynisfjall**, the high ridge above Vík, Rte 215 leads 5km down to the black-sand beach at Reynisfjara. The raw beach is backed by an incredible stack of **basalt columns** that look like a magical church organ and there are outstanding views west to Dyrhólaey. The surrounding cliffs are pocked with caves formed from twisted basalt, and puffins bellyflop from here into the crashing sea during the summer. Immediately offshore are the towering sea stacks **Reynisdrangur**.

Sögusetrið MUSEUM

3 ◉ Map p90, A3

Hvolsvöllur's Saga Centre is devoted to the dramatic events of *Njál's Saga*, which took place in the surrounding hills. Interactive displays explain the many highlights of the story. In 2013 an intricate 90m embroidery called **Njál's Saga Tapestry** (www.njalurefill.is; ◷10am-6pm Tue-Sat Jun-Aug, reduced hours Sep-May) was begun; visitors can pay to add stitches (Ikr1000) to the enormous collaborative project, or just observe. There's also a longhouse **cafe** and **tourist information** (brochures, maps and helpful staff). (Saga Centre;

Local Life

Stokkseyri & Eyrarbakki

South of the Ring Road, approximately 45km west of Hella, the tiny fishing villages of Stokkseyri and Eyrarbakki are refreshingly local-feeling. Stokkseyri has summertime art galleries and **Draugasetrið** (Ghost Centre; www.draugasetrid.is; Hafnargata 9; adult/child Ikr2000/1000, incl Icelandic Wonders Ikr3500/1500; ◷1-6pm Jun-Aug), a veritable haunted house run by a gaggle of bloodthirsty teens. In Eyrarbakki, **Flói Nature Reserve** is super for birdwatching and duelling restaurants **Við Fjöruborðið** (☎483 1550; www.fjorubordid.is; Eyrabraut 3a; mains Ikr2600-5550; ◷noon-9pm Jun-Aug, from 5pm Sep-May; ☎) and **Rauða Húsið** (☎486 8701; www.raudahusid. is; Búðarstígur 4; mains Ikr1900-3500; ◷11.30am-9pm Mon-Thu, to 10pm Fri-Sun; ☎) contend for the 'best lobster bisque' award.

Basalt columns on the beach at Vík

487 8781; www.njala.is; Hlíðarvegur 14, Hvolsvollur; adult/child Ikr900/free; ⊙9am-6pm mid-May–mid-Sep, 10am-5pm Sat & Sun mid-Sep–mid-May)

Skógar Folk Museum
MUSEUM

4 ⊙ Map p90, B4

The highlight of little Skógar is the wonderful Skógar Folk Museum, which covers all aspects of Icelandic life. The vast collection was put together by 91-year-old Þórður Tómasson over more than 75 years. There are also restored buildings (a church, a turf-roofed farmhouse, cowsheds etc), and a huge, modern building houses an interesting transport and communication museum, cafe

Local Life
Horse Riding

Many horse farms around the south, especially near Hella and Hvolsvöllur, and between Skógar and Vík, offer rides or multiday tours, and most have accommodation. Expect to pay Ikr6500 to Ikr9000 for a one-hour ride, and up to Ikr13,000 for a three-hour ride, though prices can drop for groups. Outfitters include **Herríðarhóll** (487 5252; www.herridarholl.is; Herríðarhóli), **Hekluhestar** (487 6598; www.hekluhestar. is; Austvaðsholt) and **Skálakot** (487 8953; www.skalakot.com).

Understand

Icelandic Volcanoes

Situated on the Mid-Atlantic Ridge, a massive 18,000km-long rift between two of the earth's major tectonic plates, Iceland is a shifting, steaming lesson in classroom geology. A mere baby in geological terms, it's the youngest country in Europe, formed by underwater volcanic eruptions along the joint of the North American and Eurasian plates 17 to 20 million years ago. The earth's crust in Iceland is only a third of its normal thickness, and magma (molten rock) continues to rise from deep within, forcing the two plates apart. The result is clearly visible at Þingvellir (p76), where the great rift Almannagjá broadens by between 1mm and 18mm per year.

The thin crust and grating plates are responsible for a whole host of exciting volcanic activities, but fissure eruptions and their associated craters are probably the most common type of eruption in Iceland. The still-volatile Lakagígar crater row around **Mt Laki** is the country's most unearthly example. It produced the largest lava flow in human history in the 18th century, covering an area of 565 sq km to a depth of 12m.

Subglacial & Submarine Eruptions

Several of Iceland's liveliest volcanoes lie beneath glaciers, which makes for drama as molten lava and ice interact. The main eruption of **Eyjafjallajökull** in 2010 caused a *jökulhlaup* (flooding caused by volcanic eruption beneath an ice cap) before throwing up the famous ash plume that grounded Europe's aeroplanes. Iceland's most active volcano, **Grímsvötn**, which lies beneath Vatnajökull ice cap, behaved similarly in 2011.

In 1963 the island of **Surtsey** exploded from the sea, giving scientists the opportunity to study how smouldering chunks of newly created land are colonised by plants and animals. Surtsey is off-limits to visitors, but you can climb many classical-looking cones such as **Hekla**, once thought to be the gateway to Hell; **Eldfell**, which did its best to bury the town of Heimaey in 1974; and **Snæfellsjökull** (p106) on the Snæfellsnes Peninsula.

The **Icelandic Met Office** (www.vedur.is) keeps track of eruptions and the earthquakes that tend to precede them, plus the emissions that follow.

Skógakaffi (⊙10am-5pm), and a shop. (Skógasafn; ☑487 8845; www.skogasafn.is; adult/child Ikr1750/free, outside structures only Ikr800; ⊙museum 9am-6pm Jun-Aug, 10am-5pm May & Sep, 11am-4pm Oct-Apr)

Seljalandsfoss & Gljúfurárbui

WATERFALLS

5 ⊙ Map p90, B4

From the Ring Road, west of Skógar, you'll see the beautiful high falls at Seljalandsfoss, which tumble over a rocky scarp into a deep, green pool. A (slippery) path runs around the back of the waterfall. A few hundred metres further down the Þórsmörk road, Gljúfurárbui gushes into a hidden canyon. Sterna and Reykjavík Excursions buses from Reykjavík to Skógar and beyond stop at Seljalandsfoss.

Sólheimajökull

GLACIER

6 ⊙ Map p90, C4

One of the easiest glacial tongues to reach is Sólheimajökull, east of Skógar. This icy tongue unfurls from the main Mýrdalsjökull ice cap and is a favourite spot for glacial walks and ice climbing. A 4.2km rutted dirt track (Rte 221) leads off the Ring Road to a small car park and **Cafe Solheimajokull** (☑852 2052; snacks Ikr820-1500; ⊙10am-6pm May-Sep, reduced hours Oct-Apr), from where you can walk the 800m to the ice along a wide track edging the glacial lagoon. Don't attempt to climb onto the glacier unguided.

Skógafoss

WATERFALL

7 ⊙ Map p90, B4

The 62m-high waterfall Skógafoss topples over a rocky cliff at the western edge of Skógar in dramatic style. Climb the steep staircase alongside

Top Tip

Adventure Tours

South Iceland (www.south.is) is the land of adventure tours. Most local operators offer lots of combinations and Reykjavík pick-ups; most Reykjavík companies also run tours here.

South Iceland Adventures (☑770 2030; www.siadv.is) Great bespoke adventure operators: hiking, super-Jeeps, canyoning, ice climbing.

Southcoast Adventure (☑867 3535; www.southadventure.is) Excellent small operator with super-Jeeps, hiking, snowmobiling, volcano tours and glacier walks.

Icelandic Mountain Guides (☑587 9999, Skógar office 894 2956; www.mountainguide.is) Sólheimajökull glacier walks and ice climbs.

Arcanum (☑487 1500; www.arcanum.is) Daily Sólheimajökull glacier walks, ice climbing, super-Jeep, ATV and other tours.

Katla Track (☑849 4404; www.katlatrack.is) Explores landmarks near Vík and Mýrdalsjökull.

for giddy views, or walk to the foot of the falls, shrouded in sheets of mist and rainbows. Legend has it that a settler named Þrasi hid a chest of gold behind Skógafoss...

Þjórsárstofa

MUSEUM

8 ⊙ Map p90, A2

Stop in the tiny settlement of Árnes, near the junction of Rtes 30 and 32, for the informative Þjórsárstofa. In the large white building, it has an excellent free surround-sound-style film about the Þjórsárdalur river valley and what you will see further along. There are multimedia displays and a good restaurant as well. (Þjórsá Visitor Centre; 486 6115; www.thjorsarstofa.is; admission free; ⊙10am-6pm Jun-Aug)

Eyjafjallajökull Visitor Centre

EXHIBITION

9 ⊙ Map p90, B4

This centre, about 7km west of Skógar, is on a farm on the southern flanks of Eyjafjallajökull which was impacted by the 2010 eruption. A 20-minute film (usually in English) tells the family's story, from the ominous warnings to the devastating aftermath of the flooding ash. Movie snippets include tender family moments and highlights from the team of local rescuers that dug the farm out. (Þorvaldseyri Visitor

---

Understand

Skaftafell & Vatnajökull National Park

Vatnajökull National Park (Map p90, G1; www.vjp.is, www.visitvatnajokull.is) is the largest park in Europe, measuring 13,900 sq km – nearly 14% of the entire country. **Skaftafell**, the jewel in the park's crown, encompasses a breathtaking collection of peaks and glaciers. It's Iceland's favourite wilderness: 300,000 visitors per year come to marvel at thundering waterfalls, twisted birch woods, tangled rivers threading across the sandar, and brilliant blue-white Vatnajökull with its enormous ice tongues. There are around 30 of these outlet glaciers, pleated with crevasses, with many visible (and accessible, to varying degrees) from the Ring Road in the southeast.

The great year-round **Skaftafell Visitor Centre** (Skaftafellsstofa; 470 8300; www.vjp.is; ⊙8am-9pm Jun-Aug, 9am-7pm May & Sep, 10am-5pm Mar-Apr & Oct, 11am-4pm Nov-Feb; ⊛) has exhibitions and a small cafe, and information on walks, like the 1.8km one to **Svartifoss** (Black Falls), a stunning, moody-looking waterfall flanked by geometric black basalt columns. **Icelandic Mountain Guides** (IMG; Reykjavík 587 9999, Skaftafell 894 2959; www.mountainguide.is) and **Glacier Guides** (Reykjavík 571 2100, Skaftafell 659 7000; www.glacierguides.is) lead glacier walks and adventure tours.

Vatnajökull National Park

Center – Iceland Erupts; ☑487 8815; www. icelanderupts.is; Þorvaldseyri; adult/child Ikr750/free; ☺9am-6pm Jun-Aug, 10am-4pm May & Sep, 11am-4pm Oct-Apr)

Atlantsflug   FLIGHTSEEING

10 ◉ Map p90, A4

From Bakki Airport, on the coast 5km northwest of Landeyjahöfn, Atlants- flug offers 30-minute to 75-minute overflights (Ikr22,300 to Ikr44,000) of Eyjafjallajökull, glaciers and high- lands. Flights also run to Heimaey, in the Vestmannaeyjar (one-way Ikr8000), and depart from Skaftafell and Reykjavík. (☑854 4105; www. flightseeing.is)

Eating

Gamla Fjósið   ICELANDIC €€

Built in a former cowshed that was in use until 1999, the focus of this charming eatery, west of Skógar (see 9 ◉ Map p90, B4), is on farm-fresh and grass-fed meaty mains – from burgers to Volcano Soup, a spicy meat stew. The hardwood floor and low beams are cheered with polished dining tables, large wooden hutches and cheerful staff. (Old Cowhouse; ☑487 7788; www.gamlafjosid.is; Hvassafell; mains Ikr1100- 6500; ☺11am-9pm Jun-Aug, reduced hours Sep-May; ☺)

Suður-Vík
ICELANDIC, ASIAN €€

11 Map p90, D5

The friendly ambience, from hardwood floors and interesting artwork to smiling staff, helps elevate this new restaurant in Vík beyond the competition. Food is Icelandic hearty, from heaping steak sandwiches with bacon and Bearnaise sauce to Asian (think Thai satay with rice). In a warmly lit silver building atop town. Book ahead in summer. (☑487 1515; Suðurvíkurvegur 1, Vík; mains Ikr1750-4950; ⊙noon-10pm)

Local Life
Vestmannaeyjar

The Vestmannaeyjar (Westman Islands) form 15 eye-catching silhouettes off the shore. **Heimaey** (Map p90, A4) is the only inhabited island, and its town lies between escarpments and volcanoes (part of a 1973 eruption that almost covered the village). Heimaey is famous for its 10 million puffins, the Þjóðhátíð festival and its excellent museum, **Eldheimar** (Pompeii of the North; ☑488 2000; www. eldheimar.is; Gerðisbraut 10; adult/10-18 yr/under 10yr Ikr1900/1000/free; ⊙11am-6pm Jun–mid-Sep, reduced hours rest of year). It's a great day trip on ferry **Herjólfur** (☑481 2800; www.eimskip.is; adult/child/car/bicycle Ikr1260/630/2030/630). **Slippurinn** (☑481 1515; www.slippurinn.com; Strandvegur 76; mains Ikr2000-3900; ⊙5.30-11pm Sun-Thu, to 1am Fri & Sat; 🛜) serves top meals.

Halldórskaffi
INTERNATIONAL €€

Inside Brydebúð museum in Vík (see 11 Map p90, D5), this lively timber-lined all-rounder is very popular in high season for its crowd-pleasing menu ranging from burgers and pizza to lamb fillet. The coffee is a decent brew. Book ahead or prepare to wait in summer. On weekend nights it stays open later as a bar. (☑487 1202; www. halldorskaffi.is; Víkurbraut 28, Vík; mains Ikr3000-5500; ⊙11am-9pm Jun-Aug, reduced hours Sep-May)

Hótel Skógafoss
ICELANDIC €€

The bistro-bar at Hótel Skógafoss in Skógar (see 7 ⊙ Map p90, B4) is one of the best eating and drinking spots in town, with plate-glass windows looking onto the falls and local beer on tap. (☑487 8780; www.hotelskogafoss.is; mains Ikr1200-2300; ⊙11am-9.30pm Jun-Sep)

Hellubíó
INTERNATIONAL €€

12 Map p90, A3

This large silver roadhouse in Hella, with bright potted flowers out front, stands out for its simple menu of local food ranging from lobster soup to burgers, plus draught beer, friendly staff and excellent chocolate cake. (☑853 7777; Þrúðvangur 32; mains Ikr2000-5000)

Eldstó Art Café
CAFE €€

Eldstó (see 3 ⊙ Map p90, A3) offers fresh-brewed coffee, homemade daily specials (like coconut curry soup) and a couple of outdoor Ring Road-side tables. The owners are ceramicists, and also offer

Landmannalaugar & Þórsmörk Trekking

Mind-blowing multicoloured rhyolite mountains, soothing hot springs, rambling lava flows and clear blue lakes make **Landmannalaugar** one of Iceland's most unique destinations. The area is the starting point for the famous multiday **Laugavegurinn hike**, and there's some excellent **day hiking** as well. The popular 55km Laugavegurinn leads south to the hidden valley of **Þórsmörk** (*thors*-mork; literally 'Thor's forest') at the dramatic confluence of several larger river-carved valleys. A nature reserve, Þórsmörk is a verdant realm of forest and flower-filled lees that looks onto curling gorges, icy rivers and three looming glaciers (Tindfjallajökull, Eyjafjallajökull and Mýrdalsjökull). Its lovely setting and proximity to Reykjavík (130km) make it a popular spot in summer. Þórsmörk may seem relatively close to the Ring Road on a map (and it is the better destination for those short on time), but you'll need to take a bus or go by high-clearance 4WD (super-Jeep tour!) to ford the rivers on the way to the reserve. Or hike in on the **Fimmvörðuháls** trail from Skógar.

accommodation upstairs. (www.eldsto.is; Austurvegur 2, Hvolsvöllur; mains Ikr1390-2700; ☺8am-10pm Jun-Aug; 🛜)

Þjórsárstofa Restaurant   ICELANDIC €€

The Þjórsárstofa in Árnes (see 8 ⊙ Map p90, A2) has a good restaurant with an ever-changing menu of regional cuisine and local beers. (Matstofan; www.thjorstofa.is; mains Ikr950-3200; ☺9am-9pm Jun-Aug; 🛜)

Shopping

Víkurprjón   SOUVENIRS

The big 24-hour souvenir and knitwear shop next to the N1 petrol station in Vík (see 11 ❌ Map p90, D5) is a coach-tour hit. Swing in to watch woolly jumpers being made on-site. (Austurvegur 20, Vík; ☺24hr)

Top Experiences
Jökulsárlón

Getting There

🚗 Car Makes overnighting easy.

🚌 Bus Reykjavík–Höfn Sterna bus 12/12a; Strætó bus 51; Reykjavík Excursions bus 15 (Skaftafell Visitor Centre) and bus 19 (Höfn–Skaftafell).

One of Iceland's most magical sights, Jökulsárlón glacier lagoon is filled with spectacular, luminous-blue icebergs drifting out to sea. The hours will zip by as you're wowed by wondrous ice sculptures (some striped with ash from volcanic eruptions) as they spin in the changing light; or go scouting for seals or take a boat trip. The icebergs calve from Breiðamerkurjökull, an offshoot of Vatnajökull. Though it's right beside the Ring Road (between Höfn and Skaftafell), it's 375km from Reykjavík, so warrants sleeping over in the south.

Don't Miss

The Lagoon

Although it looks as though it's been here since the last ice age, the lagoon is only about 80 years old. Until the mid-1930s **Breiðamerkurjökull** reached the Ring Road; it's now retreating rapidly (up to a staggering 500m per year), and the lagoon is growing. Icebergs can spend up to five years floating in the 25-sq-km-plus, 260m-deep lagoon before they travel via Jökulsá, Iceland's shortest river, out to sea.

Boat Tours

Take a memorable 40-minute trip with **Glacier Lagoon Amphibious Boat Tours** (☑478 2222; www. icelagoon.is; adult/child Ikr4000/1000; ⊘9am-7pm Jun-Aug, 10am-5pm Apr-May & Sep-Oct), which trundle along the shore like buses before driving into the water. It also offers Zodiac tours, as does **Ice Lagoon Zodiac Boat Tours** (☑860 9996; www. icelagoon.com; adult/child Ikr6500/4900; ⊘9am-5.30pm mid-May–mid-Sep), which speed up to the glacier edge (not done by the amphibious boats) before cruising back slowly. Check online for details and to book ahead.

Wildlife

Keep a look-out for seals bobbing up in the lagoon between the brilliant bergs. The zooming Arctic terns nest not only on the shore but also on some of the larger ice chunks!

The River Mouth

Visit the river mouth where you'll see ice boulders resting photogenically on the black-sand beach as part of their final journey out to sea.

---

admission free

⊘24hr

☑ Top Tips

▶ Summer nights can be glowing golden.

▶ On the Ring Road west of the car park, parking areas have trails to less-touristed shoreline.

▶ Local guide Thor offers **glacier hikes** (☑866 3490; www.icewalk. is; tours Ikr12,500) on Breiðamerkurjökull.

✗ Take a Break

The **cafe** (⊘9am-7pm Jun-Aug, 10am-5pm Sep-May) beside the lagoon has snacks. **Þórbergssetur** (www.thorbergur.is; adult/child Ikr1000/free; ⊘9am-8pm), a museum and cultural centre 12km east of the lagoon, has a quality cafe-restaurant. Accommodation, such as **Hali Country Hotel** (☑478 1073; www.hali. is; d with/without bathroom incl breakfast from Ikr32,200/20,800; 🛜), surrounds it.

Explore

West Iceland

Geographically close to Reykjavík yet far, far away in sentiment, west Iceland (Vesturland; www.west.is) is a splendid microcosm of what Iceland has to offer. Snæfellsjökull National Park is great for birding, whale watching, lava-field hikes and horse riding. An exceptional museum in lively Borgarnes illustrates local Sagas. Upcountry beyond Reykholt you'll encounter lava tubes and remote highland glaciers.

The Region in a Day

☀ Spend your morning in Borgarnes learning about Iceland's Viking settlers and wild, wonderful *Egil's Saga* at the **Settlement Centre** (p104), and touring the local Saga sites like Egil's farm. Lunch at the Settlement Centre's excellent on-site **restaurant** (p113) or stroll to waterfront cafe **Edduveröld** (p114) for casual eats and great views.

☀ Next, either head inland to take a tour on enormous **Langjökull** (p111) or in Iceland's largest lava tube **Viðgelmir** (p111), or zip up the coast to the Snæfellsnes Peninsula to spend your afternoon exploring the **Snæfellsjökull National Park** (p106) and going puffin-spotting and whale-watching on **Breiðafjörður** (p109).

☽ Overnight in Stykkishólmur for its top lodgings, restaurants such as **Plássið** (p114) and interesting museums such as **Norska Húsið** (p111), which you can visit the next day, or catch some theatre at funky **Frystiklefinn** (p116) before heading back to Reykjavík.

◉ Top Experiences

Settlement Centre (p104)

Snæfellsjökull National Park (p106)

♥ Best of West Iceland

Eating
Narfeyrarstofa (p113)

Plássið (p114)

Natural Wonders
Snæfellsjökull National Park (p106)

Viðgelmir (p111)

Museums & Exhibitions
Settlement Centre (p104)

Snorrastofa (p112)

Getting There

🚗 **Car** Easiest.

🚌 **Bus** Borgarnes is the major transfer point between Reykjavík and Akureyri, Snæfellsnes and the Westfjords. **Strætó** (☏540 2700; www.bus.is) bus 57 stops en route to/from Reykjavík and Akureyri. Bus 58 goes to Stykkishólmur; you can change to bus 82 (Stykkishólmur–Arnarstapi) at the Vatnaleið crossroads to go to western Snæfellsnes. Bus 81 serves Reykholt. **Sterna** (☏551 1166; www.sterna.is) bus 60/60a travels to/from Reykjavík.

Top Experiences
Settlement Centre

Buzzy Borgarnes and its broad Borgarfjörður were the landing zone for several famous Icelandic settlers. Housed in an imaginatively restored warehouse by the harbour, the fascinating Settlement Centre offers insights into the history of Icelandic settlement and brings alive the story of one of its most famous settlers, poet-warrior Egil Skallagrímsson (the man behind *Egil's Saga*), his amazing adventures and his equally intense family. The centre has also placed cairns throughout town marking key sites from *Egil's Saga*.

◉ Map p110, B4

Landnámssetur Íslands

☎ 437 1600

www.settlementcentre.is

Brákarbraut 13-15, Borgarnes

🕙 10am-9pm Jun-Sep, 11am-5pm Oct-May

Wood carving of a character from *Egil's Saga*

Don't Miss

Settlement Exhibition

The *Settlement Exhibition* vividly covers the discovery and settlement of Iceland and gives a firm historical context in which to place your Icelandic visit. The interactive map illustrating where the first settlers made inroads is particularly fun, and the audioguide's recounting of settlers' stories illustrates how harsh it all was.

Egil's Saga Exhibition

Egil's Saga is one of the most nuanced and action-packed of the Sagas, and the exhibition uses creative art and diorama displays to recount how poet-warrior Egil Skallagrímsson's family settled the Borgarnes area, and how Egil became both a fierce and sensitive man, from his near murder by his own father, to the death of his own sons.

Local Landmarks

To explore how *Egil's Saga* ties to the Borgarnes area, download the detailed **Locatify SmartGuide** (www.locatify.com; incl in Settlement Centre admission, otherwise €15) smartphone or iPad app. It tells stories of local landmarks which the Settlement Centre has marked with cairns, including **Brákin**, Egil's farm Borg á Mýrum, and **Skallagrímsgarður**, the burial mound of Egil's father and son.

Egil's Farm

Borg á Mýrum (p115), just northwest of Borgarnes on Rte 54, is where Skallagrímur Kveldúlfsson, Egil's father, made his farm at Settlement. It was named for the large **rock** (*borg*) behind the farmstead. You can walk up to the **cairn** for super views. The small **cemetery** includes an ancient rune-inscribed gravestone. Ásmundur Sveinsson's **sculpture** represents Egil mourning the death of his sons and his rejuvenation in poetry.

☑ Top Tips

▶ The museum is divided into two exhibitions; each take about a half-hour to visit. The cost for one exhibition is Ikr1900/1500 per adult/child, while two exhibitions costs Ikr2500/1900

▶ Detailed multilingual audioguides are included.

▶ Leave time to explore area sites from *Egil's Saga*.

✗ Take a Break

The Settlement Centre has a top-notch restaurant (p113) built into the rock face and serving modern Icelandic fare. Or if you feel like strolling the town, the fun waterfront Edduveröld (p114) offers a more casual cafe vibe, but equally delicious eats, and has art galleries on an upper storey.

Top Experiences
Snæfellsjökull National Park

Sparkling fjords, dramatic volcanic peaks, sheer sea cliffs, sweeping golden beaches and crunchy lava flows make up the diverse and fascinating landscape of the 100km-long Snæfellsnes Peninsula. The area is crowned by the glistening ice cap Snæfellsjökull, immortalised in Jules Verne's *Journey to the Centre of the Earth* (1864). Snæfellsjökull National Park encompasses much of the peninsula's western tip. You'll find lava tubes, protected lava fields home to native Icelandic fauna, and prime coastal bird- and whale-watching spots.

⊙ Map p108, A3

☎ 436 6860

www.snaefellsjokull.is

The coastline at Hellnar

Don't Miss

Hellnar Visitor Centre & Hikes

Hiking trails criss-cross the park, and the **Visitor Centre** (Snæfellsjökull National Park Visitor Centre; ☎591 2000, 436 6888; www.snaefellsjokull.is; admission free; ☯10am-5pm 20 May–10 Sep, reduced hours rest of year) in Hellnar sells maps (free online) and gives advice (as do area tourist offices). Rangers have summer programs of **free guided tours**. The centre has a museum on park history and wildlife.

Snæfellsjökull

It's easy to see why Jules Verne chose Snæfell for his adventure *Journey to the Centre of the Earth*: the peak was torn apart when the volcano beneath exploded. Today the crater is filled with the ice cap (highest point 1446m; *jökull* means 'glacier'). To reach its summit take a tour from Hellnar or Arnarstapi.

Öndverðarnes

At the westernmost tip of Snæfellsnes an ancient lava flow leads to Öndverðarnes Peninsula, great for **whale watching**. From the last parking area (at a squat, orange **lighthouse**), walk to the tip of the peninsula, or head 200m northeast to **Fálkí**, an ancient stone well thought to have three waters: fresh, holy and ale! The **Svörtuloft bird cliffs** (Saxhólsbjarg) are to the south.

Djúpalón Beach & Dritvík

On the southwest coast, wild black-sand beach **Djúpalónssandur** offers dramatic walks with rock formations (an elf church and **kerling**, a troll woman!), shipwreck debris and the rock-arch **Gatklettur**. Rocky **sea stacks** emerge from the ocean as you tramp north over the craggy headland to reach black-sand **Dritvík**, once the largest Icelandic fishing station, now lonely ruins.

☑ Top Tips

▶ Dress warmly and wear hiking boots and gloves if you're taking a (much-loved) 45-minute guided tour of the fascinating **Vatnshellir Lava Cave** (☎665 2818; www.vatnshellir.is; tours adult/child Ikr2500/1000).

▶ Stykkishólmur, on the peninsula's northern coast, is the region's largest town and a good base for overnighting.

▶ Even the well-trained and -outfitted are not allowed to ascend the glacier without a local guide; contact the National Park Visitor Centre in Hellnar, or take a tour.

✗ Take a Break

Hellnar Visitor Centre has the small, welcoming **Primus Café** (☎865 6740; mains Ikr1390-1980; ☯10am-9pm) for simple meals. Fjöruhúsið (p114), by the rocky waterfront, serves soups and coffees with a wonderful view over seabird nests and the shore.

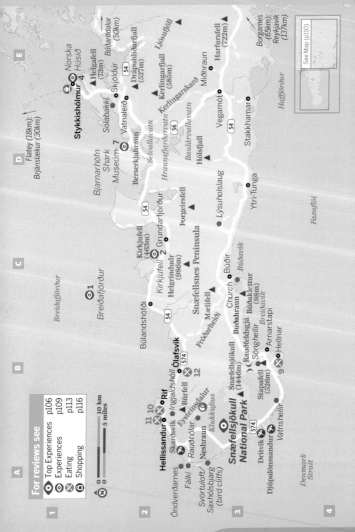

0 5 miles
0 10 km

See Map (p110)

Flatey (18km);
Brjánslækur (30km)

Breiðafjörður

Breiðafjörður

Búðardalur (50km)

Norska
Húsið
Helgafell (73m)
Stykkishólmur 4
Skjöldur
Sólabakki
Vatnaleið
Drápuhlíðarfjall (527m)
Ljósufjöll
Harðarfell (722m)
Borgarnes (65km);
Reykjavík (137km)
Bjarnarhöfn Shark Museum 7
Berserkjahraun
Selvallavatn
Hraunsfjarðarvatn
Kerlingarfjall (585m)
Kerlingarskarð
Miðhraun
Haffjörður
Bílandshöfði
Kirkjufell (463m)
Kirkjufell 2
Grundarfjörður
Þorgeirsfell
Baulárvallavatn
Hólsfell
Vegamót
Stakkhamar
Snæfellsnes Peninsula
Helgrindur (986m)
Lýsuhólslaug
Ytri-Tunga
Faxaflói
Ólafsvík
Birfell
12
Rif
Hellissandur
11 10
Skarðsvík
Ingjaldshóll
Eysteinsdalur
Klukkufoss
Fróðárheiði
Mælifell
Búðir
Church
Búðahraun
Búðaklettur (88m)
Búðavík
Breiðavík
Snæfellsjökull (1446m)
Snæfellsjökull National Park
Stapafell (526m)
Rauðfeldsgjá
Sönghellir
Arnarstapi
Hellnar
9
Öndverðarnes
Fálki
Rauðhólar
Neshraun
Svörtuloft/
Saxhólsbjarg (bird cliffs)
Dritvík
Djúpalónssandur
Snæfellsjökull
Vatnshellir

Denmark Strait

Kirkjufell

Experiences

Breiðafjörður

FJORD

1 ◎ Map p108, C1

Stykkishólmur's jagged peninsula pushes north into stunning Breiðafjörður, a broad waterway separating the Snæfellsnes from the looming cliffs of the distant Westfjords. According to local legend, there are only two things in the world that cannot be counted: the stars in the night sky and the craggy islets in the bay. You *can* count on epic vistas and a menagerie of wild birds (puffins, eagles, guillemots etc). Take **boat trips**, including whale watching and puffin viewing, from Stykkishólmur, Grundarfjörður and Ólafsvík.

Kirkjufell

MOUNTAIN

2 ◎ Map p108, C2

Kirkjufell (463m), guardian of Grundarfjörður's northern vista, is said to be one of the most photographed spots in Iceland. You'll see Ben Stiller skateboarding past in *The Secret Life of Walter Mitty* (2013). Ask the Saga Centre if you want to climb it (around €40 for a guide). Two spots involving a rope climb make it dangerous to scale when wet or without local knowledge.

Kirkjufell is backed by the roaring waterfalls, **Kirkjufellsfoss**; more camera fodder.

See Map (p108)

10 km
20 miles

Eiríksjökull
(1675m)

Hallmundarhraun

Haftafell
(1167m)

Langjökull

Geitlandsjökull
(1390m)

Þórisjökull
(1350m)

Kaldidalur Corridor

F578

Surtshellir &
Stefánshellir

Viðgelmir

Langjökull

Ice Cave

Húsafell

Ok
(1190m)

551

550

Flóstunga

Hraunfossar

Barnafoss

Kaldá

Tvídægra

Arnarvatnsheiði

1

Snorrastofa Reykholt

519

Delidartunguhver

Kleppjárnsreykir

Flókadalur

Fossatún

Hvítá

50

52

508

Skorradalsvatn

68

Staðarskáli

586

Haukadalsá

Haukadalur

1

Baula
(934+m)

Hraunsnef

60

Grábrók

Birfröst

1

Munaðarnes

Svignaskarð

50

50

Eiríksstaðir

Stóra-
Vatnshorn

Erpsstaðir

60

Laxárdalur

59

Höskuldsstaðir

Búðardalur

60

Fellströnd

Hvammsfjörður

54

BORGARBYGGÐ

Langavatn

Hítarvatn

539

55

Hlíðarvatn

54

540

533

13

Hvanneyri

53

Hafnarfjall

8

Borgarnes
Settlement
Centre

Borg á
Mýrum

Hítardalur

Borgarfjörður

54

Viðgelmir
LAVA TUBE

3 ⊙ Map p110, D3

East of Húsafell, along Rte 518, the vast lava flows of **Hallmundarhraun** make up a wonderful eerie landscape dotted with gigantic lava tubes. The easiest to visit, and the largest in Iceland, 1100-year-old, 1.5km-long Viðgelmir is located on private property near the farmstead **Fljótstunga**. It sparkles with ever-changing ice formations. You can't visit on your own, but the friendly family at Fljótstunga offer 90-minute tours during summer (10am, noon, 3pm and 5pm), by reservation in winter. (🖉435 1198; www.fljotstunga.is; campsites per person Ikr1000, cottages from Ikr8000, tours Ikr3000; ⏲May-Sep; 🛜)

Norska Húsið
MUSEUM

4 ⊙ Map p108, E1

Stykkishólmur's quaint maritime charm comes from the cluster of wooden warehouses, shops and homes orbiting the town's harbour. Most date back about 150 years. One of the most interesting (and oldest) is the Norska Húsið, now the regional museum. Built by trader and amateur astronomer Árni Thorlacius in 1832, the house has been skilfully restored and displays a wonderfully eclectic selection of local antiquities. On the 2nd floor you visit Árni's home, an upper-class 19th-century residence, decked out in his original wares.

The museum also hosts occasional **art exhibitions**. (Norwegian House; 🖉433 8114; www.norskahusid.is; Hafnargata 5; admission Ikr800; ⏲noon-5pm Jun-Aug)

Langjökull Ice Cave
CAVE

5 ⊙ Map p110, D3

At the time of research, work was under way on digging an enormous 300m-long tunnel and series of caves, at 1260m above sea level, into Langjökull glacier. Slated to open in May 2015, the tunnel and caves will contain exhibitions, a cafe and a small chapel – yes, for those who want to tie the knot inside a glacier. Tours can be had (March to October) from Húsafell or the glacier edge (Ikr17,900), or from Reykjavík (Ikr29,900) with the possibility of looping in the Golden Circle. (www.icecave.is; ⏲Mar-Oct)

Local Life
A Climb & A Soak

A favourite Snæfellsnes hike is up roadside scoria crater **Saxhöll**, which was responsible for some of the lava on the western side of the peninsula. From the base it's an uneven 300m climb for magnificent views over the enormous **Neshraun** lava flows. Then head east over to **Lýsuhólslaug** (Map p108, C3; admission Ikr550; ⏲1-8pm Jun–mid-Aug), where a geothermal source pumps in carbonated, mineral-filled waters at a perfect 37°C to 39°C. Don't be alarmed that the pool is a murky green: the iron-rich water attracts some serious algae.

Snorrastofa

MUSEUM

6 👁 Map p110, C3

The interesting medieval study centre Snorrastofa is devoted to celebrated medieval poet, historian and statesman Snorri Sturluson, and is built on his old farm in Reykholt, where he was brutally slain. The centre houses displays explaining Snorri's life and accomplishments, including a 1599 edition of his *Heimskringla* (sagas of the Norse kings). There's also material on the laws, literature and society of medieval Iceland, and on the excavations of the site. You can ask to see the modern church and reading room upstairs. (📞 433 8000; www.snorrastofa.is; Reykholt; admission Ikr1200; ⏰ 10am-6pm May-Aug, to 5pm Mon-Fri Sep-Apr)

Local Life

Stykkishólmur

The charming town of Stykkishólmur (Map p108, E1), the largest on the Snæfellsnes Peninsula, is built around a natural harbour tipped by a basalt islet. It's a picturesque place with a laid-back attitude and a sprinkling of brightly coloured buildings from the late 19th century, featured in Ben Stiller's *The Secret Life of Walter Mitty* (2013). With a comparatively good choice of accommodation and restaurants, and transport links, Stykkishólmur makes an excellent base for exploring the region.

Bjarnarhöfn Shark Museum

MUSEUM

7 👁 Map p108, D2

The farmstead at Bjarnarhöfn is the region's leading producer of *hákarl* (fermented shark meat), a traditional Icelandic dish. The museum has exhibits on the history of this culinary curiosity, along with the family's fishing boats and processing tools. A video explains the butchering and fermenting procedure: Greenland shark, which is used to make *hákarl*, is poisonous if eaten fresh. Fermentation neutralises the toxin. Note: Greenland shark is classified Near Threatened.

Find the museum off Rte 54 on the fjord-side, northeastern edge of Berserkjahraun.

Each visit to the museum comes with a bracing nibble of *hákarl*, accompanied by *brennivín*, 'black death' schnapps. Ask about the drying house out back. You might find hundreds of dangling shark slices drying; the last step in the process. (📞 438 1581; www.bjarnarhofn.is; admission Ikr1000; ⏰ 9am-8pm Jun-Aug, reduced hours Sep-May)

Volcano Museum

MUSEUM

The Volcano Museum (see 4 👁 Map p108, E1), housed in Stykkishólmur's old cinema, is the brainchild of vulcanologist Haraldur Sigurðsson, and features art depicting volcanoes, plus a small collection of interesting lava ('magma bombs'!) and artefacts from eruptions. A film screens upstairs.

Stykkishólmur harbour

You can book a full-day geology tour (Ikr17,000) around the Snæfellsnes Peninsula with Haraldur. (Eldfjallasafn; ☎433 8154; www.eldfjallasafn.is; Aðalgata 8, Stykkishólmur; adult/child Ikr800/free; ⏲11am-5pm May-Sep)

Eating

Narfeyrarstofa   ICELANDIC €€

This charming restaurant in Stykkishólmur (see 4 ⊙ Map p108, E1), run by an award-winning chef known for his superlative desserts, is the Snæfellsnes' darling fine-dining destination. Book a table on the 2nd floor to dine under gentle eaves and the romantic lighting of antique lamps. Ask your waiter about the portraits on the wall – the building has an interesting history. (☎438 1119; www.narfeyrarstofa.is; Aðalgata 3, Stykkishólmur; mains Ikr3600-5100; ⏲noon-10pm Apr–mid-Oct, 6-10pm Sat & Sun mid-Oct–Mar; ✒)

Settlement Centre Restaurant   INTERNATIONAL €€

8 ✗ Map p110, B4

The Settlement Centre's restaurant, which is in a light-filled room built into the rock face, is airy, upbeat and one of the region's best bets for food. You can choose from traditional Icelandic and international eats (such as lamb, fish stew etc). The lunch buffet (noon to 3pm; Ikr2100) is very popular. You'll need to book ahead for dinner. (☑437 1600; Brákarbraut 13, Borgarnes; mains Ikr2400-5600; ⏱10am-9pm; 🤏)

Top Tip

Tours

Láki Tours (☑546 6808; www.laki-tours.com) Puffins, whales and fishing from Grundarfjörður or Ólafsvík.

Seatours (Sæferðir; ☑433 2254; www.seatours.is; Smiðjustígur 3, Stykkishólmur; ⏱8am-8pm mid-May–mid-Sep, 9am-5pm mid-Sep–mid-May) Boat tours, including much-touted 'Viking Sushi', around Breiðafjörður.

Iceland Ocean Tours (☑517 5555; www.icelandoceantours.is; Hafnargata 4, Stykkishólmur; tours from Ikr5200, bicycle hire per day Ikr3000; ⏱Apr-Sep) Zodiac cruises around Breiðafjörður.

Go West! (☑695 9995; www.gowest.is) Biking, hiking and glacier tours.

Snæfellsjökull Glacier Tours (☑663 3371; www.theglacier.is; snowcat/snowmobile tours Ikr11,000/25,000; ⏱Mar-Jul) Snowcats/snowmobiles on Snæfellsjökull.

Lýsuhóll (☑435 6716; www.lysuholl.is; d/q incl breakfast Ikr18,500/30,000, cottage Ikr20,000) Horse riding in southern Snæfellsnes.

Stóri Kambur (☑852 7028; www.storikambur.is) Horse riding in southern Snæfellsnes.

Plássið

ICELANDIC, BISTRO €€

The newest creation of the owners of Narfeyrarstofa, this bistro-style old-town building in Stykkishólmur (see 4 ⊙ Map p108, E1) is the perfect family-friendly spot, with elegant touches (wine glasses, mod furnishings) and friendly service. Using local ingredients, they serve up a full run of regional specials, and the catch of the day is usually delicious, paired with salad or barley risotto. Local beers, too. (☑436 1600; www.plassid.is; Frúarstígur 1, Stykkishólmur; mains Ikr1400-4200; ⏱11.30am-3pm & 6-10pm; 🖊🧒)

Edduveröld

CAFE €€

Casual and friendly, with a wonderful waterfront deck, Edduveröld (see 8 ❌ Map p110, A4) is the newest entry in Borgarnes for delicious homemade dishes, from super cakes to full meals of roast lamb or fresh fish. (☑437 1455; www.edduverold.is; Skúlgata 17; mains Ikr700-4200; ⏱10am-9pm Sat-Thu, to 1am Fri; 🤏🖊)

Fjöruhúsið

SEAFOOD, CAFE €€

9 ❌ Map p108, B3

It's well worth following the stone path down to the ocean's edge for the renowned fish soup at quaint Fjöruhúsið in Hellnar. Beautifully situated by the bird cliffs at the trailhead of the scenic Hellnar–Arnarstapi path, it also serves coffee in sweet, old-fashioned china. (☑435 6844; Hellnar; mains Ikr2300-2800, cake Ikr950; ⏱10am-10pm Jun-Aug, reduced hours Apr-May & Sep-Oct)

Understand
Egil's Saga

Icelanders hold west Iceland in high regard for its canon of local Sagas. The famous *Egil's Saga* starts with the tale of Kveldúlfur, grandfather of warrior-poet Egil Skallagrímsson (sometimes spelt Egill), who fled to Iceland during the 9th century after a falling out with Norway's king. Kveldúlfur grew ill on the journey, and instructed his son, Skallagrímur Kveldúlfsson, to throw his coffin overboard after he died and build the family farm wherever it washed ashore – this happened to be at **Borg á Mýrum** (Rock in the Marshes). Egil Skallagrímsson grew up to be a fierce and creative individual who killed his first adversary at the age of seven, went on to carry out numerous raids on Ireland, England and Denmark, and saved his skin many a time by composing eloquent poetry. Learn about him at Borgarnes' Settlement Centre (p104).

It is thought that one of the most important medieval chieftains and scholars, Snorri Sturluson (1179–1241), may have written *Egil's Saga*. The Snorrastofa (p112) museum explores his legacy in sleepy inland hamlet, Reykholt.

Gamla Rif
CAFE €

10 Map p108, B2

Gamla Rif is run by two fishermen's wives who have perfected a variety of traditional snacks. They dispense local travel tips with a smile, and serve tasty coffee and cakes. They also make a mean fish soup (from their husbands' daily catch) with fresh bread, if you're feeling peckish. (📞436 1001; Háarifi 3, Rif; cakes from Ikr850, fish soup Ikr1900; ⏰noon-8pm Jun-Aug)

Hótel Hellissandur Restaurant
ICELANDIC €€

11 Map p108, B2

Hótel Hellissandur boasts a friendly staff running its consistently yummy restaurant, which serves Icelandic staples, plus burgers and the like. (📞430 8600; www.hotelhellissandur.is; Klettsbuð 7, Hellissandur; mains Ikr1790-4900; ⏰11.30am-9.30pm Jun-Sep)

Hótel Hellnar Restaurant
ICELANDIC €€

Even if you're not overnighting at Hótel Hellnar, we highly recommend having dinner at its restaurant (see 9 Map p108, B3) which sources local organic produce for its Icelandic menu. It also offers heavenly *skyr* cake for dessert. Make sure to book ahead. (Hótel Hellnar, Hellnar; dinner mains Ikr3450-4950; ⏰6-9.30pm May-Sep)

Hraun
INTERNATIONAL €€

12 Map p108, B2

This new establishment on the main road in Ólafsvík cheerfully fills a blonde-wood building with a broad front deck. The only gig in town besides fast food, it does excellent fresh mussels, burgers and fish, and has beer on tap. (📞 431 1030; Grundarbraut 2, Ólafsvík; mains Ikr2000-5000; ⊙noon-midnight daily Jun-Aug, noon-2pm Mon-Thu, noon-midnight Fri-Sun Sep-May; 🛜)

Drinking

Sjávarpakkhúsið
CAFE, BAR €€

This old fish-packing house in Stykkishólmur has been transformed into a wood-lined cafe-bar (see 4 ◎ Map p108, E1) with harbourfront outdoor seating.

◯ Local Life

Favourite Trails: Between Arnarstapi & Hellnar

Local maps detail myriad hiking trails connecting the sights of the Snæfellsnes Peninsula. One of the most popular (and scenic!) is the 2.5km coastal walk (around 40 minutes) between Hellnar and Arnarstapi (Map p108, B3, B3). This slender trail follows the jagged coastline, going through a nature reserve and passing lava flows and eroded stone caves. In tumultuous weather waves spray through the rocky arches; when it's fine, look for nesting seabirds.

The speciality is blue-shell mussels straight from the bay, but it's also a great daytime hang-out. On weekend evenings it turns into a popular bar where locals come to jam. (📞 438 1800; Hafnargata 2, Stykkishólmur; mains Ikr2750-5000; ⊙noon-10pm Sun-Thu, to 3am Fri & Sat Jun-Aug, reduced hours Sep-May; 🛜)

Entertainment

Frystiklefinn
THEATRE, LIVE MUSIC €

This quirky new joint in Rif (see 10 🍽 Map p108, B2) combines austere six-bed dorms (Ikr4600) with a cool theatre and live-music venue. In summer there's an active program of plays, storytelling and music. Check online for the schedule, and for winter opening. (📞 865 9432; www.frystiklefinn.is; Hafnargata 16, Rif)

Shopping

Ljómalind
MARKET

A recent collaboration between local producers, this packed farmers market sits at the edge of Borgarnes (see 8 🍽 Map p110, B4) near the roundabout. It stocks everything from fresh dairy products from **Erpsstaðir** (📞 843 0357; www.erpsstadir.is; admission to cowshed adult/child Ikr600/free; ⊙1-5pm Jun–mid-Sep; 👪) and organic meat, to locally made bath products, handmade wool sweaters, jewellery and all manner of imaginative collectables. (Farmers' Market; 📞 437 1400; www.ljomalind.is; Sólbakka 2, Borgarnes; ⊙11am-6pm Jun-Aug, reduced hours rest of year)

ANAÞÓRINA MELLOR/GETTY IMAGES ©

Traditional Icelandic woollen sweaters

Ullarselið
CLOTHING, ARTS & CRAFTS

13 🔒 Map p110, B4

Find your way to off-the-beaten path village Hvanneyri, 12km east of Borgarnes, and in among fjord-side homes you'll find this fantastic wool centre. Handmade sweaters, scarves, hats and blankets share space with skeins of beautiful handspun yarn, and interesting bone and shell buttons. Plus there are needles and patterns to get you started. (📞437 0077; www.ull.is; Hvanneyri; ⊗noon-6pm Jun-Aug, 1-5pm Thu-Sat Sep-May)

Leir 7
ARTS & CRAFTS

Artist Sigríður Erla produces tableware from the fjord's dark clay at this pottery studio in the heart of Stykkishólmur (see 4 ◉ Map p108, E1). (www.leir7.is; Aðalgata 20, Stykkishólmur; ⊗2-5pm)

The Best of
Reykjavík

Reykjavík Roasters (p61)
ICELANDIC PHOTO AGENCY/ALAMY ©

Best Walks
Historic Reykjavík

🏃 The Walk

The earliest signs of settlement in Reykjavík date to just before 871 and are centred in the Old Reykjavík quarter. Norwegian Viking Ingólfur Arnarson is credited with being the country's first permanent inhabitant. He made his home in a promising-looking bay that he named Reykjavík (Smoky Bay), after the steam from its thermal springs. This walk takes in the highlights of Ingólfur's historic neighbourhood.

Start Kraum

Finish National Museum

Length 1.6km; 1½ hours

✕ Take a Break

Stop for a coffee on Austurvöllur square, or across the street at smart bistro Nora Magasin (p32), for a quick tipple or a more substantial meal. Celebrity chef Völundur Völundarson conceived the creative menu.

Fríkirkjan í Reykjavík & the National Gallery of Iceland (p55)

MARK SALTER/ALAMY ©

❶ Kraum

Reykjavík's oldest timber house dates to 1762, and sits on Aðalstræti, one of the capital's oldest streets. The house is now home to **Kraum** (p36), one of the first stores showcasing Icelandic art and design.

❷ Reykjavík 871 +/-2: The Settlement Exhibition

Beneath **Reykjavík 871 +/-2: The Settlement Exhibition** (p26) lies a 10th-century Viking longhouse, which was discovered and excavated in 2001 when the hotel next door was renovated. Curators have recreated the dimly lit mood of the longhouse but have tricked it out with multimedia displays bringing the era to life.

❸ Skúli Magnússon Statue

Across from the Settlement Exhibition, there's a **statue** of powerful town magistrate-sheriff Skúli Magnússon (1711–94), who organised the building of weaving, tanning and wool-dyeing factories in the capital –

the foundations of the modern city of Reykjavík.

❹ Austurvöllur

Grassy **Austurvöllur** (p31) was once part of settler Ingólfur Arnarson's hay fields. It sits next to the **Alþingi** (parliament; p31) and in its centre there's a statue of Jón Sigurðsson (1811–79), who led the campaign for Icelandic independence. The adjacent cathedral, **Dómkirkja** (p32), was built in the 18th century.

❺ Iðnó

As you approach lake Tjörnin, you'll see the waterside **Ráðhús** (city hall; p31). Inside there's a fun topographical map of Iceland. **Iðnó** (Iðnaðarmannahúsið; The Craftsmen's House) was designed and built by Einar Pálsson in 1896 and was the city's main meeting hall, and for many years a theatre.

❻ Around Tjörnin

As you make your way around **Tjörnin** (p29), which is called 'The Pond', by locals, you'll

pass the quaint church, **Fríkirkjan í Reykjavík**, the **National Gallery of Iceland** (p55) and **Hljómskálagarður Park** (p29), which contains sculptures by five historic Icelandic artists.

❼ National Museum

The **National Museum** (p24) traces human history in Iceland, from the earliest settlement to the modern era. There are also rotating photographic exhibits and a welcoming cafe.

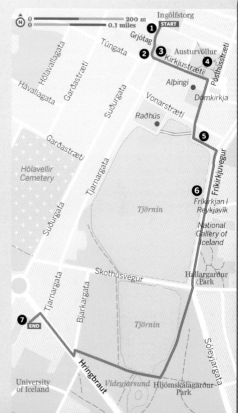

Best Walks
Reykjavík Art & Design

🏃 The Walk

Icelanders have a knack for piquant, arresting art and design. The city is littered with local creations, including modernist architecture, cool contemporary art, and shops full of functional but creative crafts and design gadgets. This walk takes you through a sampling of the disciplines, all in a compact, popular section of central Reykjavík.

Start Reykjavík Art Museum – Kjarvalsstaðir

Finish Harpa concert hall

Length 3km; two hours

🍴 Take a Break

Stop for a delicious, organic meal at Gló (p58), where the menu changes daily and is accompanied by a broad bar of intricate and flavourful salads. A colourful crew of locals crowds in for popular lunches, and plenty of bars and coffee shops sit just nearby.

KLAUS LANG/GETTY IMAGES ©

Harpa concert hall (p55)

❶ Reykjavík Art Museum – Kjarvalsstaðir

The **Kjarvalsstaðir** (p55) looks onto Miklatún Park, and is named for Jóhannes Kjarval (1885–1972), one of Iceland's most popular classical artists. The peaceful museum displays his wonderfully evocative landscapes and also the works of many major 20th-century Icelandic painters.

❷ Einar Jónsson Museum

Einar Jónsson (1874–1954) was one of Iceland's foremost sculptors, with his dramatic allegorical style. The **Einar Jónsson Museum** (p56) fills the studio he designed. Upper stories have city views; the **sculpture garden** (p56) behind it is free.

❸ Hallgrímskirkja

Guðjón Samúelsson (1887–1950), perhaps Iceland's most renowned 20th-century architect, created a distinctive Icelandic aesthetic. Reykjavík's **Hallgrímskirkja** (p50) is perhaps the pinnacle of his work. Pop around the corner to classic 1937 swimming pool, **Sundhöllin** (p57), to see another example.

4 Design Shops

Icelandic artists and designers create many objects that combine beauty and practicality. Laugavegur is loaded with shops selling designers' work. To the east, **Kiosk** (p63) is a couture cooperative. **KronKron** (p63) has top clothes, but their handmade shoes are off the charts. **Leynibúðin** (p64) sells hip locally crafted apparel. To the west, tiny **Skúma Skot** (p64) is packed with unique handmade art and clothing.

5 Art

Walk to the ocean's edge for the popular *Sun-Craft* sculpture, stopping off at **Kling & Bang** (p56), one of the city's top galleries for emerging artists. **Sun-Craft** (p57) itself was created by Jón Gunnar Árnason, and its skeletal ship-like frame sits powerfully along the water, with snow-topped mountains in the distance.

6 Harpa Concert Hall

Reykjavík's dazzling **Harpa concert hall** (p55), with its facade of glimmering hexagons, opened in 2011 and was designed by Danish firm Henning Larsen Architects, Icelandic firm Batteríið Architects, and Danish-Icelandic artist Olafur Eliasson. Be sure to zip inside to see its vaulted glass panels and wonderful harbour sightlines.

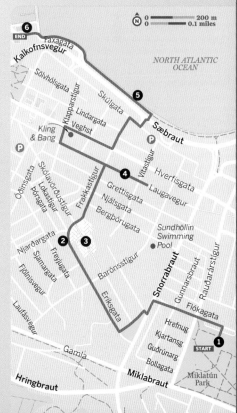

Best
Eating

Yes, Icelanders love hot dogs, and there are boundary-pushing dishes like fermented shark or sheep's head. But the spotlight shines brightest on Iceland's delicious, fresh-from-the-farm ingredients, seafood bounty from its icy waters, innovative dairy products (don't miss *skyr*) or the clever historic food-preserving techniques finding new favour with today's much-feted New Nordic chefs.

Food Culture

Reykjavík is not only the political but also the culinary capital of Iceland. Choices range from a vibrant cafe-bar scene, where effortlessly cool Reykjavikers hang out sipping fine coffees and munching sandwiches, cakes and waffles, to top-of-the-heap New Nordic restaurants, taking Icelandic cuisine to its most rarefied extremes.

Icelandic Specialities

If you see a queue in Reykjavík, it probably ends at a *pýlsur* (hot dog) stand. *Fiskisúpa* (fish soup) comes courtesy of family recipes, while *kjötsúpa* (meat soup) will usually feature veggies and chunks of lamb. Icelandic lamb is hard to beat, with free-range sheep munching chemical-free grasses and herbs in the highlands and valleys.

In the past, Icelanders merely kept the cheeks and tongues of *þorskur* (cod) – a delicacy – and exported the rest, but today you'll commonly find cod fillets on the menu, along with *ýsa* (haddock), *bleikja* (Arctic char) and meaty-textured *skötuselur* (monkfish). During the summer you can try *silungur* (freshwater trout) and *villtur lax* (wild salmon). There's also wild-caught animals such as whale, *hákarl* (fermented shark), reindeer and *lundi* (puffin).

NEIL JOHN SMITH/GETTY IMAGES ©

☑ Top Tips

▶ Reserve ahead in summer for top restaurants.

▶ Even in summer, restaurants may stop serving around 9pm.

▶ Be aware there are conservation issues regarding whales, puffins and sharks (see boxed text, p45).

Best Food on the Go

Bæjarins Beztu
Reykjavík's most legendary hot-dog stand. (p32)

Lobster Hut Get your lobster on the go...as a sandwich or salad. (p35)

Soup Car Lamb stew and vegan soup next to Hallgrímskirkja. (p60)

Grillmarkaðurinn (p32)

Walk the Plank Crab sliders portside in the Old Harbour. (p45)

Hamborgara Búllan Reykjavík's favourite burgers. (p47)

Best Fine Dining

Dill One of Reykjavík's finest restaurants. (p57)

Þrír Frakkar Top Icelandic dishes in a cosy dining room. (p58)

Grillmarkaðurinn Trendy and tops for steaks and grilled fish. (p32)

Fiskfélagið Fresh Icelandic seafood flavoured with far-out spices. (p32)

Fiskmarkaðurinn Exquisite Icelandic tasting menus. (p34)

Kolabrautin Icelandic meets Italian atop Harpa concert hall. (p59)

Best Restaurants Outside Reykjavík

Narfeyrarstofa in Stykkishólmur, run by an award-winning chef. (p113)

Plássið Reliably delicious seafood and burgers in Stykkishólmur. (p114)

Lindin Lakeside in Laugarvatn, with fantastic wild-caught mains. (p86)

Slippurinn In Heimaey, with a lively vibe, overlooking the harbour. (p98)

Silfra Near Þingvellir, slow-food local ingredients and a bar. (p77)

Gamla Fjósið West of Skógar, in an old cowshed, with farm-raised beef. (p97)

Best Local

Tíu Droppar The 'Ten Drops' effortlessly combines cafe, bar and restaurant. (p60)

Ostabúðin Open only for lunch, the 'Cheese Shop' dishes up the owner's catch of the day. (p59)

Grái Kötturinn Tiny, hard to find, but great for breakfasts and brunch. (p58)

Við Fjöruborðið Oceanside seafood in Stokkseyri with yummy lobster bisque. (p92)

Vitabar Scrumptious burgers in a Reykjavík bar. (p62)

Best Veg-Organic

Gló Fresh, organic and loaded with tasty herbs and spices. (p122)

Grænn Kostur Organic and vegan specialities. (p59)

Best
Cafes & Bars

The city's ratio of coffeehouses and bars to citizens is nothing short of staggering. Handcrafted caffeine hits and designer microbrews are prepared with the utmost seriousness for accidental hipsters sporting well-worn *lopapeysur* (Icelandic woollen sweaters). In fact, the local social scene is built around low-key cafes that crank up the intensity after hours, when tea is swapped for tipples and dance moves break out.

Best Cafes

Babalú Great for tasty baked goods and a kitschy vibe. (p60)

Reykjavík Roasters Premier coffee aficionados roast their own beans. (p61)

Kaffi Mokka One of the capital's oldest cafes with an approachable, well-worn feel. (p61)

Café Haiti In the Old Harbour, with coffee sourced from Haiti. (p47)

C is for Cookie Tiny and in a relaxed residential neighbourhood, it's totally untouristy. (p61)

Best Cocktail Bars

Loftið Top-shelf all the way, with a jazzy retro feel. (p35)

Slippbarinn Old Harbour's top fancy drinks place, with food too. (p47)

Best Local

Kaffibarinn A Reykjavík institution, which is chilled by day and packed on weekend nights. (p53)

Kaldi Effortlessly cool with its own microbrews on tap. (p52)

Prikið A quintessential dive bar with good stick-to-your-ribs diner food. (p53)

Boston The arty crowd hangs out here; it's above Laugavegur. (p53)

Dillon Rock bar with frequent live music. (p53)

Best Streetside People-Watching

Bravó Local beer on tap and good happy hours on a busy Laugavegur corner. (p61)

Café Paris On the edge of Old Reykjavík's Austurvöllur square; grab a drink and watch the action. (p34)

Best Beer Selection

Micro Bar Rotating selection of 10 beers on tap, and a good happy hour. (p35)

Best Late-Night

Húrra Six beers on tap and an enormous back room that opens up for live music most nights. (p36)

Paloma After-hours dancing, DJs and a pool table. (p35)

Best
Museums, Exhibitions & Galleries

Best Art Museums

Reykjavík Art Museum Three wonderful branches included in one ticket: downtown Hafnarhús (p29) focusing on contemporary art; Kjarvalsstaðir (p55) with 20th-century art; and Ásmundarsafn (p67) for sculptures by Ásmundur Sveinsson.

National Gallery of Iceland Constantly changing lakeside collection of Iceland's finest artists. (p55)

Reykjavík Museum of Photography Annual exhibitions of primarily Scandinavian photography. (p31)

Sigurjón Ólafsson Museum Oceanside sculpture with sea breezes, totem poles and busts. (p67)

Best History Museums

National Museum All of Iceland's best artefacts gathered under one well-curated roof. (p24)

Reykjavík 871 +/-2: The Settlement Exhibition Excellent multimedia exhibits and an excavated Viking longhouse. (p26)

Settlement Centre Borgarnes' interesting examination of Settlement and one of the Sagas of the time, *Egil's Saga*. (p104)

Sögusetrið Hvolsvöllur's museum dedicated to the local *Njál's Saga*. (p92)

Snorrastofa Reykholt farmstead of celebrated medieval poet, historian and statesman Snorri Sturluson. (p112)

Best Off-Beat Museums & Exhibitions

Icelandic Phallological Museum Fascinating, yes fascinating, array of Icelandic penises – all of the mammals are represented. (p55)

Draugasetrið Goulish haunted house in Stokkseyri, with spooky tales and dried ice. (p92)

Saga Museum Silicon models and dioramas bringing the gory, thrilling hijinks of Settlement to life. (p43)

Best Natural Phenomena

Volcano House Watch movies of Icelandic volcanoes erupting. (p31)

Aurora Reykjavík Learn about and watch a simulation of the Northern Lights. (p44)

Best Art Galleries

i8 Famous Icelandic and international contemporary artists. (p31)

Kling & Bang Young up-and-comers in the art world. (p56)

Best
Tours

Reykjavík makes a superb base camp for loads of regional tours to the wild outdoors. Whether you're simply not up for renting your own wheels, or you want to head to areas that require expert guidance or serious equipment, you'll find a tour to suit almost any timeframe, need or skill level. Many regional operators also pick up from Reykjavík.

Reykjavík Tours

The tourist office has free maps and self-guided walking tour brochures, and info on guided walking tours. You can buy the more in-depth *Reykjavík Walks* (Guðjón Friðriksson; 2014) at local bookshops. There are several downloadable smartphone apps, including two by **Locatify** (www.locatify.com). For a list of whale- and puffin-spotting tours see p40.

Best Reykjavík Tours

Literary Reykjavík (www.bokmenntaborgin.is; Tryggvagata 15; ⏲3pm Thu Jun-Aug) Free literary walking tours start at the main library. *Literary Reykjavík* app.

Free Walking Tour Reykjavik (www.freewalkingtour.is; ⏲noon & 2pm Jun-Aug, reduced in winter) One-hour, 1.5km walking tour of the centre.

City Sightseeing Reykjavík (📞580 5400; www.city-sightseeing.com; adult/child Ikr3500/1750; ⏲hourly 10am-6pm Jun–mid-Sep) Hop-on, hop-off bus taking in all major sights around town starting at Harpa.

Best Bicycle Tours

Reykjavík Bike Tours & Segway Tours (📞694 8956; www.icelandbike.com; Ægisgarður 7, Old Harbour; bike rental per 4hr from Ikr3500, tours from Ikr5500; ⏲9am-5pm Jun-Aug, reduced hours Sep-May) Bike hire and tours of Reykjavík and countryside.

Bike Company (📞590 8550; www.bikecompany.is; Bankastræti 2, Reykjavík; bike rental per 5hr Ikr3500; ⏲9am-5pm Mon-Fri) Bicycle tours and hire.

Best Bus Tours

Reykjavík Excursions (Kynnisferðir; 📞580 5400; www.re.is; Vatnsmýrarvegur 10, BSÍ bus terminal) Most popular bus operator. Lots of summer and winter programs.

Iceland Excursions (Gray Line Iceland; 📞540 1313; www.grayline.is; Hafnarstræti 20) Large

Horse riding near Landmannalaugar (p99)

groups on comprehensive day trips.

Sterna (☎551 1166; www.sterna.is; Harpa Concert Hall; ☻7am-6.30pm) More modest-sized operator.

Gateway to Iceland (☎534 4446; www.gatewaytoiceland.is) Smaller groups and good guides.

Go Green (☎694 9890; www.gogreen.is) Small and high-end with sustainable practices.

Best Adventure Tours

Arctic Adventures (☎562 7000; www.adventures.is; Laugavegur 11; ☻8am-10pm) Young, enthusiastic action-filled tours.

Icelandic Mountain Guides (☎587 9999; www.mountainguides.is; Stórhöfði 33) Full-action outfit

specialising in mountaineering, ice climbing etc.

Mountaineers of Iceland (☎580 9900; www.mountaineers.is) Excellent guides, lots of super-Jeep, and snowmobiling tours, including heli-snowmobiling.

Inside the Volcano (☎863 6640; www.insidethevolcano.com; admission Ikr37,000; ☻mid-May–Sep) Amazing trip into a perfectly intact 4000-year-old magma chamber.

Best Horse-Riding Tours

Eldhestar (☎480 4800; www.eldhestar.is; Vellir, Hveragerði) Established horse farm near Hveragerði.

Íshestar (☎555 7000; www.ishestar.is; Sörlaskeið 26, Hafnarfjörður) One of the

largest, oldest stables; rides through lava fields.

Laxnes (☎566 6179; www.laxnes.is; Mosfellsbær) On the way out to Þingvellir.

Best Air Tours

Eagle Air Iceland (☎562 4200; www.eagleair.is; Reykjavík Domestic Airport) Sightseeing flights over volcanoes and glaciers.

Air Iceland (☎570 3030; www.airiceland.is; Reykjavík Domestic Airport) Combination air, bus, hiking, rafting, horse riding etc day tours around Iceland.

Atlantsflug (☎854 4105; www.flightseeing.is; Reykjavík Domestic Airport) Flightseeing tours from Reykjavík, Bakki Airport and Skaftafell.

Best
Natural Wonders

It is an absolute must to take a day trip or an overnight outside of Reykjavík to take in some of the incredible volcanic landscapes, geothermal fields, glaciers, dramatic fjords and black-sand seashores. In summer, bird life can be abundant, with puffins flapping and Arctic terns diving. And from October to April look for the Northern Lights.

MARK HAMBLIN/GETTY IMAGES ©

Best Volcanoes

Hekla Once thought to be the gates of hell; you can climb it. (p94)

Eyjafjallajökull Blew an enormous ash cloud and stopped air traffic in Europe in 2010. (p96)

Eldfell Small, and brilliant sienna, it almost smothered Heimaey in lava in 1973. (p94)

Reykjanes Peninsula Four volcanic chains in action. (p72)

Best Glaciers

Vatnajökull The largest ice cap in Europe with glacier tongues and a giant park to match. (p96)

Langjökull Site of the new Ice Cave in West Iceland. (p111)

Snæfellsjökull So awesome it has a national park established for it in west Iceland. (p106)

Sólheimajökull Easily accessible ice tongue from Mýrdalsjökull ice cap. (p95)

Best Waterfalls

Gullfoss Iceland's marquee waterfall, the 'Golden Falls' course over rock tiers and down a gorge. (p80)

Seljalandsfoss You can walk behind the spraying curtain of this dramatic cascade. (p95)

Skógafoss Dreamy and huge; just to the west of Skógar. (p95)

Svartifoss Skaftafell's dramatic falls drop from black basalt columns. (p96)

Best Lava Tubes

Viðgelmir Iceland's largest lava tube, accessible by guided tour; in west Iceland. (p111)

Vatnshellir Much-loved lava tube in west Iceland's Snæfellsjökull National Park. (p106)

Best Geothermal Springs

Blue Lagoon Vibrant turquoise and world-famous. (p71)

Gamla Laugin This newly refurbished natural historic spring is located in meadows. (p83)

Fontana Chic; lakeside in Laugarvatn. (p83)

Lýsuhólslaug Bubbly water on the south coast of the Snæfellsnes Peninsula. (p111)

Laugardalslaug Reykjavík's historic springs, now a giant bathing complex. (p67)

Best **With Kids**

Best Parks

Reykjavík Zoo & Family Park What's not to love? Farm animals, floaty rafts, kids' ride, all in a grand park. (p67)

Tjörnin Get your crumbs and feed the ducks at the pretty lake. (p29)

Hljómskálagarður Examine interesting sculptures throughout the park. (p29)

Hverasvæðið Boil an egg in the thermal vents in Hveragerði. (p83)

Best Experiences

Hallgrímskirkja Take the elevator to the top of the church for thrilling views. (p50)

Whales of Iceland Look at amazing life-size replicas of all the Icelandic whales. (p44)

Volcano House Watch movies of exploding volcanoes. (p31)

Aurora Reykjavík Try out the Northern Lights simulator. (p44)

Saga Museum See silicon representations of the Sagas, then dress up in costume for photos. (p43)

Best Swims

Laugardalslaug Giant pool complex with water slide. (p67)

Blue Lagoon Teal water and silica mud for horse-play. (p71)

Gamla Laugin Huge, warm geothermal pool by a burbling stream. (p83)

Best Day Trips

Whale Watching Cruise the icy waters in search of leaping whales. (p40)

Viðey Island Bike and hike on a windswept coastal island. (p68)

Geysir Watch the geyser shoot water wonderfully high. (p78)

River Rafting Strap 'em in for a zip down the Hvítá river. (p86)

MAGNUS HJORLEIFSSON/GETTY IMAGES ©

☑ **Top Tips**

▶ Children's admission to museums and swimming pools varies from 50% to free. They pay adult fees at anywhere from 12 to 18.

▶ Kids usually get 50% off or more with bus and tour companies.

Horse Riding Take a ride on an Icelandic pony. (p93)

Best Food

Bæjarins Beztu Reykjavík's favourite hot dogs. (p32)

Valdi's Homemade ice cream and happy families. (p44)

Best
Shopping

Reykjavík's vibrant design culture and craft-oriented ethos makes for great shopping: from edgy fashion and knitted *lopapeysur* (Icelandic woollen sweaters) to unique music and loads of lip-smacking liquor. Many artists and designers form collectives and open shops and galleries full of handmade, beautiful work: everything from striking bowls made out of radishes to fish-skin handbags, creative toys and cool couture.

Design

The **Iceland Design Centre** (www.icelanddesign.is) promotes local designers' work, and you can check online for the latest news, exhibitions and events, as well as interesting blog posts. Its online Reykjavík Design Guide lists designers (from architects to ceramicists) and area shops, and its DesignMarch annual event opens hundreds of exhibitions and workshops to the public.

Sweaters & Knitting

Hand- or machine-made *lopapeysur* and other wool products are staples of Icelandic life as are many souvenir shops. Individual regions have their own motifs; for example, Borgafjörður designs feature geese, ptarmigan or salmon. Handmade garments made from local wool don't come cheap. Prices in the countryside can be lower than in Reykjavík, and you'll know the true knitting stores because they also sell yarn, patterns and needles.

Icelandic Culture and Craft Workshops (p57) offer half-day knitting workshops. Designer Hélène Magnússon offers knitting tours (www.icelandic-knitter.com) that take in spinning, wool work, design, folklore and hiking/sightseeing.

Best Fashion

Kiosk Local designers of women's clothing. (p63)

KronKron From international couture to Scandi designers, and handmade shoes. (p63)

Leynibuðin Local designers with a grunge aesthetic. (p64)

66° North Premier outdoor clothes. (p64)

Annaranna Low-key local fashion house with trendy clothing and accessories. (p65)

Gaga Fun-loving pastiches of knit and felted wool. (p37)

Volcano Wearable, original designs. (p65)

Best Design

Kirsuberjatréð A Reykjavík institution, with high-end excellent arts and crafts. (p36)

KronKron (p63)

Kraum All manner of gadgets, gewgaws and garb. (p36)

Skúma Skot Small, with bits of everything, all handmade. (p64)

Spark Art gallery meets design store where exhibits rotate and it's all for sale. (p64)

Fabúla The Old Harbour's most interesting shop with art, jewellery and some clothes. (p47)

Best Knitting & Knitwear

Handknitting Association of Iceland Two city-centre shops full of knits; the Skólavörðustígur 19 location also has supplies. (p63)

Álafoss Lots of local knits; plus a big store in Mosfellsbær. (p64)

Ullarselið In a tiny village, 12km east of Borgarnes. (p117)

Víkurprjón In Vík and open 24 hours; it also demonstrates knitting machines. (p99)

Best Souvenirs

Iceland Giftstore Large, airy and loaded with higher-end mementos, art and Icelandic fashion. (p36)

Viking Packed with trinkets and tourists. (p65)

Best Music

Lucky Records Low-key and off the beaten path, but packed with rare grooves. (p63)

12 Tónar Famous, casual store, fun for hanging out. Also a branch in Harpa. (p63)

Best Local

Frú Lauga Farmers market with products from all over Iceland. (p67)

Kolaportið Flea Market Secondhand toys sit alongside fermented shark at Reykjavík's weekend market. (p36)

Ljómalind Borgarnes' awesome farmers market. (p116)

Mál og Menning Loiter over coffee and browse in this large independent bookshop. (p63)

Best Liquor

Keflavík International Airport Duty free shops in the airport's arrivals hall. (p17)

Vínbúðin The national liquor store chain is the only game in town. (p46)

Best
Festivals

AGE FOTOSTOCK/ALAMY ©

Icelanders celebrate festivals with gleeful enthusiasm. While Reykjavík is the epicentre of the excitement, even small villages have their own festivities: for local heroes, civic pride or just good, old-fashioned quirky traditions. Almost everyone participates, and a spirit of good cheer usually applies. The Reykjavík festivals are also a super showcase for Icelandic and international music and art. Gather round and join in!

Best Music Festivals

Iceland Airwaves
(www.icelandairwaves.is) Since the first edition of Iceland Airwaves in 1999, this fab November festival has become one of the world's premier annual showcases for new music (Icelandic and otherwise).

Þjóðhátíð (www.dalurinn.
is) In Heimaey, Vestmannaeyjar, on the August long weekend, more than 11,000 people descend to watch bands and fireworks, and drink gallons of alcohol.

Secret Solstice (www.
secretsolstice.is) New in 2014 (with headliners Massive Attack), this festival co-incides with the solstice, so there's

24-hour daylight too. Held at Laugardalur in Reykjavík.

ATP Iceland (www.
atpfestival.com) Headlined by Portishead and Nick Cave in 2013 and 2014, it's back in 2015 at Ásbrú, near Keflavík.

Skálholt Summer Concerts (www.sumartonleikar.
is) The cathedral at the historic religious centre of Skálholt hosts around 40 concerts, lectures and workshops from July to August.

Reykjavík Jazz Festival
(www.reykjavikjazz.is) From mid-August, Reykjavík toe-taps its way through a week dedicated to jazz, man. Local and international musicians blow their own trumpets at events staged at Harpa.

Best Arts Festivals

Reykjavík Arts Festival
(www.listahatid.is) Culture vultures flock to Iceland's premier cultural festival in late May or early June for two weeks of local and international theatre performances, film, dance, music and visual art.

Reykjavík Culture Night (Menningarnótt;
www.menningarnott.is) Mid-August, Reykjavíkers turn out for a day and night of art, music, dance and fireworks. Galleries, ateliers, shops, cafes and churches stay open until late.

DesignMarch (www.
designmarch.is) The local design scene is celebrated at this four-day feast of all things aesthetically pleasing: from fashion to furniture, architecture to food design.

Secret Solstice music festival

Reykjavík International Film Festival (www.riff. is) Intimate 11-day event from late September features quirky programming that highlights independent film-making, both home-grown and international.

Best Cultural Festivals

National Day The country's biggest holiday commemorates the founding of the Republic of Iceland on 17 June 1944 with parades and general patriotic merriness.

Reykjavík Pride (www. reykjavikpride.com) Out and proud since 1999, this festival brings Carnival-like colour to the capital on the sec-

ond weekend of August. About 90,000 people (over one-quarter of the country's population) attended 2014's Pride march and celebrations.

Þorrablót This Viking midwinter feast (late January to mid/late February) is marked nationwide with stomach-churning treats such as *hákarl* (fermented shark), *svið* (singed sheep's head) and *hrútspungar* (rams' testicles). All accompanied by shots of *brennivín* (a potent schnapps nicknamed 'black death').

Food & Fun (www. foodandfun.is) In February, international chefs team up with local restaurants and vie for awards at this capital feast.

Verslunarmannahelgi The first weekend in August is a public-holiday long weekend when Icelanders flock to rural festivals, family barbecues, rock concerts and wild campground parties.

Seafarers' Day (Sjó-mannadagurinn) Fishing is integral to Icelandic life, and Seafarers' Day is party time in fishing villages. On the first weekend in June, every ship in Iceland is in harbour and all sailors have a day off. Salty-dog celebrations on the Sunday include drinking, rowing and swimming contests, tugs-of-war and mock sea rescues.

Best
For Free

Best Natural Wonders

Þingvellir Iceland's original parliament site, in a dramatic rift valley. (p76)

Geysir Watch the geothermal water spout like clockwork. (p78)

Gullfoss The famous Golden Falls tumble down a narrow canyon. (p80)

Reynisfjara Gorgeous black-sand beach near Vík with basalt columns, caves, puffins and sea stacks. (p92)

Dyrhólaey Photogenic rock arch off the coast of Vík, with seabird breeding grounds. (p92)

Seljalandsfoss Explore behind falls thundering next to the Ring Road. (p95)

Snæfellsjökull National Park Ice caps, lava fields, native flora and coastal walks (some led by rangers, for free). (p106)

Jökulsárlón Jaw-dropping glacial lagoon with icebergs like floating sculptures. (p100)

Best Art & Architecture

Hallgrímskirkja Wander the church grounds and look inside, though the tower will cost ya. (p50)

Viðey Island Art installations such as Yoko Ono's *Imagine Peace Tower*, Ólafur Eliasson's *The Blind Pavilion* and Richard Serra's *Milestones*. (p68)

Einar Jónsson Sculpture Garden Check out 26 bronzes in the shadow of Hallgrímskirkja. (p56)

Sun-Craft This public sculpture sits along the capital's coastline. (p57)

Harpa Wander the faceted glass interior of the monumental concert hall. (p55)

Best Local

Reykjavík Botanic Gardens Grassy fields and thousands of sub-Arctic plants and flowers. (p67)

Whale Watching in Garður Picnic on Reykjanes Peninsula head-

FLÁKUS COOKE/GETTY IMAGES ©

☑ Top Tip

▶ At the time of writing, many of Iceland's natural wonders were free but there is a government proposal to introduce a one-off fee, ensuring travellers contribute to the protection and maintenance of natural sites.

lands while watching for whales, seals and migrating seabirds. (p73)

Valahnúkur Climb the cliffs and see bubbling geothermal springs at the tip of Reykjanes Peninsula. (p73)

Reykjanesfólkvangur Wilderness Reserve Hike trails by bird cliffs, mineral lakes and multi-coloured geothermal fields. (p73)

Survival Guide

Survival Guide

Before You Go

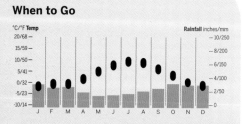

When to Go

°C/°F Temp
- 20/68
- 15/59
- 10/50
- 5/41
- 0/32
- -5/23
- -10/14

Rainfall inches/mm
- 10/250
- 8/200
- 6/150
- 4/100
- 2/50
- 0

J F M A M J J A S O N D

When to Go

➡ **High Season (Jun-Aug)** Visitors descend en masse – especially in Reykjavík and the south. Prices peak and accommodation bookings are essential. Endless daylight, plentiful festivals, busy activities.

➡ **Shoulder (May & Sep)** Breezier weather; occasional snows in interior. Optimal conditions for those who prefer smaller crowds, lower prices.

➡ **Low Season (Oct-Apr)** Long nights with possible Northern Lights viewings. Winter activities including skiing, snowshoeing, visiting ice caves.

Book Your Stay

➡ It's essential to book months ahead for June to August in Reykjavík and the southwest (especially around Vík).

➡ Reykjavík 101 is the central district, best for easy walking around town.

➡ Reykjavík has a full spectrum of accommodation: from camping and hostels to guesthouses, business hotels, apartments and boutique hotels. All book up in summer; many are open year-round.

➡ Prices are high for what you get (and rising fast). Often private apartments are the best bet.

➡ Country farmstays offer rooms, beds and/or cottages and are a fun way to overnight out of town.

Useful Websites

AirBnB (www.airbnb.com) Private rooms, apartments and houses; often the best deal in the capital.

booking.com Very popular and thorough, especially in the countryside.

Icelandic Farm Holidays (www.farmholidays.is) Top farmstays.

CouchSurfing (www.couchsurfing.com) Network travellers hosting travellers.

Lonely Planet (www.lonelyplanet.com) Author-recommendation reviews and online booking.

Best Budget

KEX Hostel (www.kexhostel.is) Reykjavík's hippest backpacker, with a lively restaurant-bar.

Reykjavík Downtown Hostel (www.hostel.is) Neat as a pin, central and friendly.

Loft Hostel (www.lofthostel.is) Trendy, central hostel with terrace bar.

Best Midrange

K Hotel (www.booking.com, booking@apartmentk.is) Artsy and on popular Laugavegur.

Guesthouse Butterfly (www.butterfly.is) Quiet, and tidy; near the Old Harbour.

Galtafell Guesthouse (www.galtafell.com) In a

peaceful converted mansion near the lake.

Villa (www.villa.is) New guesthouse in the middle of the action.

Best Top End

Hótel Borg (www.hotelborg.is) 1930s elegance with super-smart modern style.

Icelandair Hotel Reykjavík Marina (www.icelandairhotels.is) Harbour-front design hotel with small, cool rooms.

Ion Luxury Adventure Hotel (www.ioniceland.is) South of Þingvellir NP, one of Iceland's swanky country hotels.

Best Short-Stay Apartments

Reykjavík Residence (www.rrhotel.is) Plush apartments on a quiet, central street.

Room With a View (www.roomwithaview.is) Scandi-modern and deluxe, some with sea views.

Grettisborg Apartments (www.grettisborg.is) Sleek and in a central, residential neighbourhood.

REY Apartments (www.rey.is) Modern digs in the centre.

Arriving in Reykjavík

Keflavík International Airport

➔ Three easy bus services connect Reykjavík and the airport (50 minutes), and are by far the best bet; kids get discounted fares. Taxis cost approximately Ikr15,000.

Flybus (☎580 5400; www.re.is; 🛜) Operated by Reykjavík Excursions, Flybus meets all international flights. One-way tickets cost Ikr1950. Pay Ikr2500 for hotel pick-up/drop-off (which shuttles you to/from the Flybus at the BSÍ terminal); book a day ahead. A separate service runs to the Blue Lagoon (from where you can continue to the centre or the airport; Ikr3600). Tickets available online, at many hotels or at the airport booth.

K-Express (☎823 0099; www.kexpress.is) At the time of writing, K-Express offered three daily bus services running between Keflavík International Airport and Keflavík

Town, Reykjavík Camp-site, Hallgrímskirkja and the Harpa concert hall for Ikr1300. They depart (and have a desk) about 500m from the terminal, at the building with the Sixt rental-car agency. Tickets can be purchased from the bus driver or online.

Airport Express (☎540 1313; www.airportexpress. is; 📶) Operated by Gray Line Tours between Keflavík International Airport and Lækjartorg in central Reykjavík (Ikr1900), or via hotel pick-up/drop-off (Ikr2400). See website for schedule.

Reykjavík Domestic Airport

➡ From **Reykjavík Domestic Airport** (Reykjavíkurflugvöllur; www.reykjavikairport.is; Innan-landsflug) it's a 1km walk into town. There's a taxi rank, and **Strætó** (☎540 2700; www.straeto.is) bus 15 stops near the Air Iceland terminal, bus 19 stops near the Eagle Air terminal. Both go to the centre and Hlemmur bus station.

Getting Around

Local Bus

☑ **Best for...**Local travel, when you don't feel like walking.

➡ **Strætó** operates regular buses around Reykjavík and its suburbs with main stations at Hlemmur, at the eastern end of Laugavegur, and Lækjartorg.

➡ Online schedules and smartphone app. Route book for sale at Hlemmur bus station (Ikr0.50). Free maps such as *Welcome to Reykjavík City Map* also include route maps.

➡ Many buses loop around Tjörnin lake and serve the centre, National Museum, and BSÍ bus ter-minal before heading on.

➡ Fare is Ikr350; buy tick-ets at stations or pay on board (no change given). Transfer tickets (from the driver) are good for 75 minutes.

➡ One-/three-day passes (Ikr900/2200) are sold at bus stations, tourist offices, many hotels and bigger swimming pools.

➡ Buses run 7am to 11pm or midnight daily (from 10am on Sunday) at 20- or 30-minute intervals. Limited night-bus service runs until 2am on Friday and Saturday.

➡ The Reykjavík City Card (p142) also acts as a Strætó bus pass.

Car

☑ **Best for...**Countryside day trips and overnights.

➡ Totally unnecessary if you are staying in central Reykjavík.

➡ Roads are good in the most-visited areas.

➡ Book ahead for best deals; if there's two or more of you it can be cheaper than the bus.

➡ Check out **Carpooling in Iceland** (www.samferda.is

➡ Many countryside petrol stations are automated; you need a PIN-equipped ATM or credit card. Arrange one before you leave home. If you don't have a PIN, buy prepaid cards from N1 stations to use at automated pumps.

➡ 4WDs only necessary for highland travel (F roads: where 2WD rental cars are forbidden)

➡ Limited parking in the centre (Ikr120 per hour; coins and PIN-equipped

rds only). Free from
om to 10am Monday
Saturday and all day
unday.

egional Bus &
ours

Best for... Seeing the
ountryside without driv-
g, or if pinched for time.

Single or multiday
urs, many offering
otel pick-up, depart from
eykjavík (see p128), or
se Strætó and the major
us tour companies listed
ere for transport. The
ublic Transport in Iceland
ee map shows all routes.

The companies offer
us passes, but some are
ostly and you're then
ed to the one service. Do
our research: a car can
ometimes be cheaper.

From roughly mid-May
o mid-September regular
cheduled buses go to
host places on the Ring
'oad (Rte 1), into the
opular hiking areas of the
outhwest, and to larger
owns on the Reykjanes
nd Snæfellsnes Pen-
nsulas, Westfjords and
astfjords. The rest of the
ear, services range from
laily to nonexistent.

In small towns, buses
isually stop at the main
etrol station.

➡ **Strætó** (☏540 2700;
www.straeto.is) operates
Reykjavík long-distance
buses from the **Mjódd
Bus Terminal** (☏557
7854), 8km southeast
of the centre, which is
served by local buses 3,
4, 11, 12, 17, 21, 24 and 28.
Also operates city buses
and has a smartphone
app. For long-distance
buses *only* use cash,
credit/debit card with PIN
or (wads of) bus tickets.

➡ **Reykjavík Excursions**
(☏580 5400; www.re.is)
uses the **BSÍ Bus Termi-
nal** (☏562 1011; www.bsi.
is; Vatnsmýrarvegur 10; 📶),
south of the centre. BSÍ
(pronounced bee-ess-ss)
has a ticketing desk, tourist brochures, lockers,
luggage storage (Ikr500
per bag per day), Budget
car hire and a cafeteria
with wi-fi. The terminal
is served by Reykjavík

buses 1, 3, 6, 14, 15 and
19. Reykjavík Excursions
offers pre-booked hotel
pick-up to bring you to
the terminal.

➡ **Sterna** (☏551 1166; www.
sterna.is; 📶) has depar-
tures from the Harpa
concert hall (tickets
available there). Buses
go everywhere except the
west and Westfjords.

➡ **Trex** (☏587 6000; www.
trex.is; 📶) departs from
the Main Tourist Office or
Harpa concert hall and
Reykjavík Campsite. Runs
buses to Þórsmörk and
Landmannalaugar in the
south.

Air

☑ **Best for...** Quick hops
further afield.

➡ Domestic flights and
those to Greenland and
the Faroe Islands leave

Money-Saving Tips

Tax-Free Shopping Anyone with a permanent address outside Iceland can claim up to 15% refund
on purchases when they spend over Ikr4000 (at a
single point of sale). Look for stores with a 'tax-free
shopping' sign, and get a form at the register. Full
details at www.taxfreeworldwide.com/Iceland.

Alcohol Planning on drinking a lot in Reykjavík?
Buy liquor at the airport's duty free shops in the
arrivals hall to beat city prices.

from Reykjavík Domestic Airport.

➡ **Air Iceland** (📞570 3030; www.airiceland.is) operates flights and sightseeing services. Book online.

Essential Information

Discount Cards

➡ The **Reykjavík City Card** (24/48/72hr Ikr2900/3900/4900) offers free travel on the city's Strætó buses and on the ferry to Viðey, as well as free admission to Reykjavík's municipal swimming/thermal pools and to most of the main galleries and museums, and discounts on some tours, shops and entertainment.

➡ Buy the card at the tourist office, some travel agencies, 10-11 supermarkets, HI hostels and some hotels.

➡ Kids enter many museums free; the **Children's City Card** (24/48/72hr Ikr1000/2000/3000) covers other services.

Electricity

230V/50Hz

230V/50Hz

Emergency

➡ For emergency service and search and rescue call 📞112

Money

☑ **Top Tip** While credit cards are ubiquitous, many transactions (such as petrol purchases) require a PIN. Make sure you have one before you leave home.

➡ Icelandic unit of currency is the króna (plural krónur), written as Ikr here, often written elsewhere as ISK.

➡ Credit cards are used everywhere; ATMs are throughout the centre.

➡ Tipping is not required, as service and VAT (value added tax) are included.

Public Holidays

New Year's Day 1 January

Easter March or April Maundy Thursday and Good Friday to Easter Monday (changes annually)

First Day of Summer First Thursday after 18 April

Labour Day 1 May

Ascension Day May or June (changes annually)

Whit Sunday and Whit Monday May or June (changes annually)

National Day 17 June

Commerce Day First Monday in August

Christmas 24 to 26 December

New Year's Eve 31 December

Telephone
☑ **Top Tip** For longer stays, or for the mobile-addicted, Icelandic SIM cards are cheap and practical; you'll need an unlocked GSM 900/1800 mobile.

➡ Iceland's country code: ☎354 (note: Iceland has no area codes).

➡ Online phonebook: http://en.ja.is.

➡ Buy prepaid SIM cards at bookshops, grocery stores and petrol stations. Iceland telecom **Síminn** (www.siminn.is/prepaid) provides greatest network coverage; **Vodafone** (www.vodafone.is/en/prepaid) is not far behind.

➡ Voice-and-data starter packs include local SIM cards; Síminn's costs

Ikr2000 (and includes Ikr2000 in call credit).

➡ Public phones are elusive.

Tourist Information
☑ **Top Tip** Sites such as www.visitreykjavik.is and www.grapevine.is provide all you'll need for a short stay; www.visitreykjanes.is, www.south.is and www.west iceland.is cover the countryside.

Main Tourist Office
(Upplýsingamiðstöð Ferða-manna; Map p28; ☎590 1550; www.visitreykjavik.is; Aðalstræti 2; ⊙8.30am-7pm Jun–mid-Sep, 9am-6pm Mon-Fri, to 4pm Sat, to 2pm Sun mid-Sep–May) Friendly staff and mountains of free brochures, plus maps and Strætó city bus tickets for sale. Book accommodation, tours and activities. Also one site for getting your duty-free refund.

Travellers with Disabilities
➡ Iceland can be trickier than many places in northern Europe for travellers with disabilities.

➡ For details on accessible facilities, contact

the info centre for people with disabilities, **Þekkingarmiðstöð Sjálfsbjargar** (☎550 0118; www.thekkingarmidstod.is).

➡ **God Adgang** (www.godadgang.dk) can find accessible service providers.

➡ For tailor-made accessible trips: **All Iceland Tours** (www.allicelandtours.is) and **Iceland Unlimited** (www.icelandunlimited.is).

➡ Reykjavík's city buses have a 'kneeling' function so wheelchairs can be lifted on; elsewhere, buses don't have ramps or lifts.

Visas
➡ Iceland is one of 26 European Schengen Convention countries.

➡ **EU & Schengen countries** No visa required for three months.

➡ **Australia, Canada, Japan, New Zealand & USA** No visa for tourist visits up to three months. Total stay within Schengen area must not exceed three months in any period of six months.

➡ **Other countries** Check online at www.utl.is.

Language

Most Icelanders speak English, however, any attempts to speak the local language will be much appreciated. If you read our pronunciation guides as if they were English, you'll be understood.

Basics

Hello.
Halló.   ha·loh

Good morning.
Góðan daginn.   gohth-ahn dai-in

Goodbye.
Bless.   bles

Thank you
Takk./ Takk fyrir.   tak/ tak fi·rir

Excuse me.
Afsakið.   af·sa·kidh

Sorry.
Fyrirgefðu.   fi·rir·gev·dhu

Yes.
Já.   yow

No.
Nei.   nay

How are you?
Hvað segir þú gott?
kvadh se·yir thoo got

Fine. And you?
Allt fínt. En þú?   alt feent en thoo

What's your name?
Hvað heitir þú?   kvadh hay·tir thoo

My name is ...
Ég heiti ...   yekh hay·ti ...

Do you speak English?
Talar þú ensku?   ta·lar thoo ens·ku

I don't understand.
Ég skil ekki.   yekh skil e·ki

Directions

Where's the (hotel)?
Hvar er (hótelið)?   kvar er (hoh·te·lidh)

Can you show me (on the map)?
Geturðu sýnt mér (á kortinu)?
ge·tur·dhu seent myer (ow kor·ti·nu)

What's your address?
Hvert er heimilisfangið þitt?
kvert er hay·mi·lis·fan·gidh thit

Eating & Drinking

What would you recommend?
Hverju mælir þú með?
kver·yu mai·lir thoo medh

Do you have vegetarian food?
Hafið þið grænmetisrétti?
ha·vidh thidh grain·me·tis·rye·ti

I'll have a ...
Ég ætla að fá ...   yekh ait·la adh fow .

Cheers!
Skál!   skowl

I'd like a/the ..., please.   *Get ég fengið ..., takk.*   get yekh fen·gidh ..., tak

table for
borð fyrir   bordh fi·rir

bill
reikninginn   rayk·nin·gin

drink list
vínseðillinn   veen·se·dhit·lin

menu
matseðillinn   mat·se·dhit·lin

that dish
þennan rétt   the·nan ryet

Emergencies

Help!
Hjálp! hyowlp

Go away!
Farðu! far·dhu

Call ...!
Hringdu á ...! hring·du ow ...!

a doctor
lækni laik·ni

the police
lögregluna leu·rekh·lu·na

I'm lost.
Ég er villtur/villt. (m/f)
yekh er vil·tur/vilt

Where are the toilets?
Hvar er snyrtingin? kvar er snir·tin·gin

Numbers

1	*einn*	aydn
2	*tveir*	tvayr
3	*þrír*	threer
4	*fjórir*	fyoh·rir
5	*fimm*	fim
6	*sex*	seks
7	*sjö*	syeu
8	*átta*	ow·ta
9	*níu*	nee·u
10	*tíu*	tee·u
20	*tuttugu*	tu·tu·gu
30	*þrjátíu*	throw·tee·u
40	*fjörutíu*	fyeur·tee·u
50	*fimmtíu*	fim·tee·u
60	*sextíu*	seks·tee·u
70	*sjötíu*	syeu·tee·u
80	*áttatíu*	ow·ta·tee·u
90	*níutíu*	nee·tee·u
100	*hundrað*	hun·dradh

Shopping & Services

I'm looking for ...
Ég leita að ... yekh lay·ta adh ...

How much is it?
Hvað kostar þetta? kvadh kos·tar the·ta

That's too expensive.
Þetta er of dýrt. the·ta er of deert

Transport

Is this the ...
Er þetta ... er the·ta ...

to (Akureyri)?
til (Akureyrar)? til (a·ku·ray·rar)

boat
ferjan fer·yan

bus
rútan roo·tan

plane
flugvélin flukh·vye·lin

What time's
Hvenær fer ... kve·nair fer ...

the ... bus?
strætisvagninn? strai·tis·vag·nin

One ... ticket (to Reykjavík), please.
Einn miða ... (til Reykjavíkur), tak.
aitn mi·dha ... (til rayk·ya·vee·kur) takk.

How much is it to ...?
Hvað kostar til ... ? kvadh kos·tar til ...

Please stop here.
Stoppaðu hér, takk.
sto·pa·dhu hyer tak

Please take me to (this address).
Viltu aka mér til (þessa staðar).
vil·tu a·ka myer til (the·sa sta·dhar).

Behind the Scenes

Send Us Your Feedback

We love to hear from travellers – your comments help make our books better. We read every word, and we guarantee that your feedback goes straight to the authors. Visit **lonelyplanet.com/contact** to submit your updates and suggestions.

Note: We may edit, reproduce and incorporate your comments in Lonely Planet products such as guidebooks, websites and digital products, so let us know if you don't want your comments reproduced or your name acknowledged. For a copy of our privacy policy visit lonelyplanet.com/privacy.

Alexis' Thanks

My work on Reykjavík was a labour of love supported by many helping hands. At Reykjavik 871 +/-2, anthropologist Eva Dal's enthusiasm was infectious. Thanks to Jón Magnússon and Hall-grímur Stefans for double-checking my Icelandic, from *rúntur* to *djammið*. Respect to James for the astute attention he brought to the collaboration, and to Carolyn for lending her expertise.

Kristinn Viggósson rose above being a host, making Reykjavík feel like home. Yva & John became inspiring family. Ryan was, as always, a peach.

Acknowledgments

Cover photograph: Harpa concert hall and cultural centre in Reykjavík, Arctic-Images/Corbis

This Book

This 1st edition of Lonely Planet's *Pocket Reykjavík* was researched and written by Alexis Averbuck. This guidebook was produced by the following:

Destination Editor James Smart **Product Editor** Kate Kiely **Senior Cartographer** Valentina Kremenchutskaya **Book Designer** Clara Monitto **Assisting Editors** Nigel Chin, Gabrielle Stefanos

Cover Researcher Naomi Parker **Thanks to** Carolyn Bain, Samantha Forge, Elizabeth Jones, Claire Naylor, Karyn Noble, Martine Power, Alison Ridgway, Anna Tyler, Lauren Wellicome

Index

See also separate subindexes for:

🍴 Eating p150
🍸 Drinking p150
🎭 Entertainment p151
🛍 Shopping p151

Nauthólsvík beach

Kaloportid Flea Market

Icelandic Fish and Chips
Tryggvagötu 8

Reykjavik Roasters

Slippbarinn

→ Saturday & Sunday
11am → 5pm
Trygguagötu 19, Oldiharba

Our Writer

Alexis Averbuck

Alexis' love of remote, icy landscapes and untouched mountain ranges started with her year spent living in Antarctica, but now it's been fully co-opted by Iceland. A self-proclaimed glacier geek, Alexis loves exploring Iceland's remote byways: from surreal lava fields and sparkling fjords to vivid-blue glacier tongues. She also thrives on Icelandic culture, pouring over the sagas and becoming a student of Reykjavík's super music scene and excellent art and design culture. She enjoys slipping into the capital's laid-back daily life and getting to know its witty, unselfconscious residents. A travel writer for two decades, Alexis also covers Antarctica, France and Greece for Lonely Planet, has crossed the Pacific by sailboat, and is a painter – see her work at www.alexisaverbuck.com. You can also view her profile at https://auth.lonelyplanet.com/profiles/alexisaverbuck.

Published by Lonely Planet Publications Pty Ltd
ABN 36 005 607 983
1st edition – May 2015
ISBN 978 1 74321 995 9
© Lonely Planet 2015 Photographs © as indicated 2015
10 9 8 7 6 5 4 3 2 1
Printed in China